Children's Understanding their Sibling Relationships

Available in alternative formats

This publication can be provided in alternative formats, such as large print, Braille, audiotape and on disk. Please contact: Communications Department, Joseph Rowntree Foundation, The Homestead, 40 Water End, York YO30 6WP. Tel: 01904 615905. Email: info@jrf.org.uk

Children's Understandings of their Sibling Relationships

Rosalind Edwards, Lucy Hadfield and Melanie Mauthner

national
children's
bureau
making a difference

JOSEPH ROWNTREE
FOUNDATION

Joseph Rowntree Foundation
The Joseph Rowntree Foundation has supported this project as part of its programme of research and
innovative development projects, which it hopes will be of value to policy-makers, practitioners and
service users.

National Children's Bureau
NCB promotes the voices, interests and well-being of all children and young people across every aspect
of their lives. As an umbrella body for the children's sector in England and Northern Ireland, we provide
essential information on policy, research and best practice for our members and other partners.

NCB aims to:
- challenge disadvantage in childhood
- work with children and young people to ensure they are involved in all matters that
  affect their lives
- promote multidisciplinary cross-agency partnerships and good practice
- influence government policy through policy development and advocacy
- undertake high quality research and work from an evidence-based perspective
- disseminate information to all those working with children and young people, and to children
  and young people themselves.

The **Families & Social Capital ESRC Research Group** at London South Bank University focuses
on the inter-relationship between the dynamics of family change and processes of social capital.
Details of its programme of work can be found at: www.lsbu.ac.uk/families

The views expressed in this book are those of the authors and not necessarily those of the
National Children's Bureau, the Joseph Rowntree Foundation or London South Bank University.

Published by the National Children's Bureau for the Joseph Rowntree Foundation.

National Children's Bureau, 8 Wakley Street, London EC1V 7QE
Tel: 020 7843 6000.
Website: www.ncb.org.uk
Registered Charity number 258825

Contents

Acknowledgements

We would like to thank members of our Advisory Group for their constructive advice over the two years of the research project on which this report is based: Suki Ali, Simon Blake, Jenny Frank, Clem Henricson, Ginny Morrow, Ute Navidi, Bren Neale, Alison Pike and Emma Renold. We are also grateful to the Joseph Rowntree Foundation for funding the research, and especially to Susan Taylor for her support. ChildLine provided us with cards giving their UK helpline number and leaflets on bullying for primary and secondary children, for distribution to children who wanted them. Thanks to Jane Williams and Anosua Mitra for their administrative assistance, which enabled the project to run smoothly. Charlotte Ashton, Rachel Atkinson and Amanda Nicholas also helped with transcription. Olivia Thompson Edwards, age 8, provided the footnote descriptions of games and so on.

Finally, and most importantly, we want to thank the children who took part in this research, and their parents, for helping to facilitate this. They made us very welcome in their homes and the children enthusiastically engaged with our topic and the research process. In order to protect their anonymity, we asked the children to choose 'names' for themselves for us to use in writing the report. They often decided to adopt the name of their best friend, or of a popular cultural figure. Pseudonyms are also used for members of their family and friends, some of which were also provided by the children. A list of the children participating in this study is available at: www.lsbu.ac.uk/families/jrfsiblist.

1. Introduction

This report explores the views of children in 'middle childhood' – that is, aged between 7 and 13 – on their relationships with their brothers and sisters. Looking at children's sibling relationships from their own perspective is somewhat unusual because, as we discuss further below, most research on the topic is conducted from an 'outsider' rather than an 'insider' perspective. It is often concerned with investigating the relationship between the number of siblings and/or birth order and educational and behavioural outcomes, or focuses on children in families with 'problems'. In addition, attention is usually paid to strategies for dealing with sibling jealousy, arguments and other perceived difficulties in advice books for parents. The focus is on establishing generalisable 'rules' about the effects of sibling relationships and staple strategies for managing them. This approach spills over into professional practice in various ways, for example in the content of parenting skills courses, in the convention of admitting children to the same school as their older siblings, and in social work decisions about separating or keeping siblings together in care placements.

In contrast, listening to children's own accounts of their everyday life with their brothers and sisters reveals them as insightful commentators on these relationships. Their accounts provide a challenge to the predominant systematic notions about how sibling relationships work that form the current basis for research and professional practice. A key message from this study is that: **children's relationships with their siblings are complex and vary according to context, with gender and the age hierarchy as important features.** In other words, sibling relationships are both patterned and diverse; and actively constructed by children rather than given.

In this chapter we place our study of children's understandings of their relationships with their brothers and sisters in context, looking at the overall picture of sibling circumstances and previous research on sibling relationships, before laying out the aims and process of our own project.

Sibling circumstances

Statistics about the number of children living together in families are over-whelmingly collected from the point of view of the household as a unit rather than the child. In 2001, the average number of dependent children in a family was 1.8 (Office for National Statistics 2001). Just under 60 per cent of children lived in households containing more than one child, and 20 per cent of these contained three or more children. This varies by ethnic group. For example, the majority of Pakistani and Bangladeshi children lived in households containing three or more children (50 per cent), most Indian and white children lived in two-child households (45 and 40 per cent respectively), while the majority of black children (60 per cent) were evenly split between two-child households and those with three or more children (Platt 2002, Figure 4.5).

In relation to number of siblings, while there are slightly more boys than girls among dependent children as a whole (Office for National Statistics 2001), it seems that in families with more than one child in the UK, parents tend to prefer a sibling gender 'balance'. Mothers whose first two children are of the same sex are more likely go to on to have a third child, while those who have two children of different sexes are more likely to stop at two (Iacovou 2001).

The sibling-circumstances picture is further complicated, however, by family diversity – a feature that is not captured in the statistical notion of household. Marian Elgar and Ann Head (1999) identify nine different forms of sibling relationships related to family continuity or change. Parental separation and repartnering can mean that children do not necessarily live in the same household as their full biological siblings, and children may have half- or step-siblings living in the same or another household. For example, nearly one in four dependent children lives in a lone-mother family, and more than one in ten lives in a step-family (Office for National Statistics 2001), but this does not take into account that they may move between parents in different sorts of household forms. Children may also have siblings – whether full, half or step – who are no longer dependent and live outside their household. There is also evidence that, like adopted siblings, looked-after children and the children of the family with whom they are placed can regard each other as siblings (Kosonen 1999). The definition of who is a sibling may also be constructed differently between ethnic and cultural groups. For example, African-Caribbean and African families may view cousins as siblings (Chamberlain 1999; Graham 1999).

The configuration of siblings – the number of children, position in the age hierarchy, age gap and gender balance – is a focus of much research on children's relationships with their brothers and sisters, underpinned by a preoccupation with problems.

Research on siblings

There is an extensive literature on children's sibling relationships. The overwhelming majority of this work, as we noted earlier, is conducted from an 'outsider' perspective. It is parents' or teachers' reports of children that are collected, or ratings from inventories applied to children (Mullender 1999). Even where it seeks out children's own views on their sibling relationships and uses more child-focused methods, this research can still be said to take an outsider perspective in that the features of the relationship under investigation are predetermined by the researchers, rather than being grounded in the children's own perspectives.

A cornerstone of much research on siblings is in fact parents' actions. The starting point is parental childbearing, such as in the number and age difference of the children they have, and parental childrearing, and the effect that this has on child development, behavioural and educational outcomes. In a recent overview of much of the research in the sibling field in relation to educational outcomes, Lala Carr Steelman and colleagues (2002) state that a recurring finding is that the more siblings a child has, and the closer together they are in age, the more his or her educational performance and achievement decreases. This is usually explained in terms of dilution of parental resources, such as income and attention. Steelman and others argue, however, that the central, universalistic tenets of sibling research require re-evaluation because they ignore social context and meaning. Also unaddressed, including by Steelman and others, are the 'resources' that siblings may provide for each other, such as care and support.

While the evidence for the effects of sibling gender composition is said to be equivocal (Steelman, Powell, Werum and others 2002), sibling birth order is seen as having profound psychological implications into adulthood. Firstborns are said to develop dominant, conscientious and conforming personalities, and to feel resentment or ambivalence towards their younger siblings, while later-born children are risk-taking and creative, and middle children act as peacekeepers (Mitchell 2000; Sulloway 1996, 2001). Importantly, Juliet Mitchell (2003) suggests that the 'lateral' relationship between siblings is relatively autonomous and just as important as, or even more important than, 'vertical' parent–child relationships, including with respect to the construction of gender and other social demarcations.

Parents' partnering and childrearing behaviour, or the absence of parents, is another factor investigated in sibling research. Relational patterns between parents, and between parents and their children, are said to shape interactions between siblings and to account for differences between siblings growing up in the same family (Furman and McQuaid 1992; Stocker and Dunn 1994). Family change, through separation and repartnering, can both bring siblings closer together and cause conflict and feelings of displacement (Bank and Kahn 1982; Dunn and Deater-Deckard 2001). Parental socio-economic status is also featured, with sibling relationships in working-class families, especially among boys, said to become less supportive as children enter their teenage years (Dunn and Plomin 1990).

In relation to sibling bonds, generally siblings are said to be a source of both support and irritation to each other (Borland, Laybourn, Hill and others 1998). When children face conflict between parents or are separated from them, then bonds are said to be intensified, although sometimes in a harmful, over-dependent way (Bank and Kahn 1982; Kosonen 1999; Lockwood, Gaylord, Kitzmann and others 2002). Support from siblings for children who face bullying at school is also not regarded in a completely positive light, as it may increase their isolation, and siblings themselves can be a source of bullying (Duncan 1999). Another serious problem examined in relation to bonding is sibling incest (Cawson, Wattam, Brooker and others 2000; Laviola 1992). Again, such work is rarely placed in social context.

Parents are the audience for self-help books and websites, which give advice to them about 'encouraging them [siblings] to be friends' (Woolfson 2002) and 'beating the bickering between siblings' (www.raisingkids.co.uk). Sibling conflict is often understood as the result of competition for parental attention, but there are debates about its effects and remedies for it. Furthermore, the consensus of advice can change over time. While some see jealousy and fights as contributing to the development of aggression and as associated with clinical disturbance (Patterson 1986; Richman, Stevenson and Grayham 1982), others have argued that it is a normal occurrence and can also contribute more positively to the development of social understanding (Dunn 1988; Hair, Jager and Garrett 2001). Similarly, while some advocate parental intervention in sibling arguments in order to reduce tension (Kramer, Perozynski and Chung 1999; Siddiqi and Ross 1999), others have argued that this prevents children from learning how to resolve conflict (Brody, Stoneman and Burke 1987; Mok and Bromfield, undated). Questions about whether differing social contexts, and children's own interpretations of the situation, require different approaches typically remain unanswered.

In contrast to 'outsider' perspectives, there is now a growing body of work seeking to examine children's own 'insider' understandings of various aspects of their lives, and to place these in social context. While family life has been one of the concerns of this research, there has been little specific and sustained focus on sibling relationships. Nonetheless, such work does point towards the importance of their brothers and sisters for children themselves, and towards complexity of meaning in different social contexts. For example, siblings can provide each other with a sense of emotional and practical care, with age hierarchies playing a part in the flow of this caring (Brannen, Heptinstall and Bhopal 2000). Ethnicity and gender also play their part in children's conceptions of caring relationships. Children of Pakistani origin place a positive emphasis on sibling bonds (Morrow 2003), while relationships between sisters are crucial in the development of feminine subjectivity, involving fluid caring and power positions (Mauthner 2002). Gendered power relationships between siblings can also shape their access to space and other facilities in the home (McNamee 1999). A problematic view emerges from calls to the UK telephone helpline for children, ChildLine (Hall 1997; Mason 1997). Favouritism by parents, and intrusive, competitive and violent behaviour by siblings were recurring themes. While this obviously only represents children who call a telephone helpline, by its nature focusing on problems, it does give some insight into concerns and worries that children themselves identify.

Our own work seeks to extend the focus on the 'insider' perspective on children's lives. It gives full attention to, and starts from, the issues that children themselves see as key in their everyday relationships with their brothers and sisters.

Our study

Our study aimed to:

- explore how children in middle childhood understand and experience their sibling relationships, taking a child-focused approach that listens to children and treats them as experts on their own lives;
- identify the ideas and resources (material, social and psychological) that underpin children's views of their sibling relationships, what they themselves consider to be strengths and drawbacks in these relationships, and the ways that they deal with them; and
- provide information about sibling relationships in middle childhood that can make a contribution to political and professional debates about family life and

relationships, and enable the identification of potential professional strategies for support and guidance.

The research involved qualitative interviews with 58 children in middle childhood. Middle childhood is a period roughly covering 7 to 13 years old. We focused on this age group for two reasons. First, it is said to be a stage in which, among other things, children start to think more about their emotional relationships, the different social groups of people there are in the world and their own place and status (Borland, Laybourn, Hill and others 1998; Meadows 1990; Phinney 1989; Terwogt and Harris 1993). Second, children's own views of sibling relationships in middle childhood are under-researched. We do not, however, regard middle childhood as a natural and inherent 'stage' that children go through, but as one in which children are actively constructing their own understandings of their everyday lives in interaction with others (James, Jenks and Prout 1998; Mayall 2002; Morrow 1998). So our study treats children as socially competent interpreters of, and informants on, their relationships with their brothers and sisters.

Our research concentrated on everyday life with siblings for children, rather than families with problems or children who used particular services. We reached children through a nationally representative sample of parents of 8–12 year olds[1] (although we do not consider that our sample of children is representative in itself). We selected families with more than one child in their household, living in a range of metropolitan, urban and rural areas across mainland Britain. Details of our methods of accessing children and gaining consent can be found at www.lsbu.ac.uk/families/jrfsibresources, as can discussion of our ethical approach, and our flexible interview format and child-focused tools such as charts with stickers, drawing activities and short stories to comment on.

We wanted the interview process to be led by the children themselves. So, as far as possible, we tried to create an interview format that would adapt to each child's preferences and interests rather than follow a universalistic formula, and we offered them a 'menu' of topics and tools to choose from. They could select topics and activities in any order that they liked, until they wanted to stop. This allowed each child to set the pace of the interview and the balance of talk and activities.

During the interviews, we asked the children about the everyday nature of their relationships with their brothers and sisters; how they compared those relationships

---

1   The nationally representative sample of 1,112 parents was interviewed as part of a module of the NOP Parentbus survey commissioned for the 'Resources in Parenting: Access to Capitals' project being carried out under the Families and Social Capital ESRC Research Group at London South Bank University. See www.lsbu.ac.uk/families for further details. Drawing on this sample, we also included some children who were 7 and 13 in our study.

with other relationships, such as those with parents or friends; their family history memories; their daily lives, including household rules and responsibilities; their schooling; socialising with and without siblings; and whether or not they liked and disliked the same or different things as their siblings. The tape-recorded interviews were transcribed fully, and we undertook a grounded analysis of each of the children's accounts, identifying key themes in their interviews rather than searching for issues that we had identified in advance.

Sample characteristics

The 58 children in our sample came from 46 households (in 10 households we interviewed more than one child). Our sample was fairly evenly divided between boys and girls, with more children towards the younger end of middle childhood taking part (see Figure 1.1). The majority of the children were part of mixed sibling groups (containing brothers and sisters), but six of the boys had brothers only and four of the girls had sisters only. Half the children came from working-class families and half were middle class (based on parental occupation). The majority of the children were white, but a few were from minority ethnic groups: three were black, two were Asian and two were of mixed parentage. These are rather abstract and broad class and ethnic categories, but we hope that the subtle differences between these positions comes through in our in-depth discussion in this report.

Figure 1.1 Gender and age

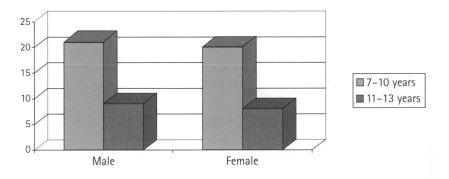

In terms of household family structures, just over half the children lived in nuclear families with both their biological parents, and a quarter lived in step-families, with the remaining children living in lone-parent families with their biological mother (see Figure 1.2). In addition, there were three children living in an extended family, who were all from one household of mixed ethnicity that contained cousins who were considered siblings, as well as two aunts.

Figure 1.2 Family form

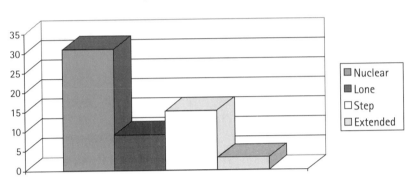

The implications of looking beyond household in addressing sibling relationships is best reflected in the number of siblings (full, half and step) for the children in our sample (see Figure 1.3). The sample is fairly evenly split between those who had one or two siblings, and those who had three or more, which is greater than the national household average noted earlier. Just under half the children had siblings living outside their family household, fairly evenly divided between those who had dependent full, half- or step-siblings living in another family household, and those with older full, half- or step-siblings living independently. Apart from three of these children (two of whom were brothers), all the others had contact with these siblings.

Figure 1.3 Number of siblings (for child)

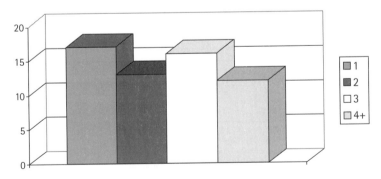

Some aspects of children's sibling circumstances make it difficult to allocate them to categories, given the complexities of family life. The 'facts' of sibling relation-ships are notably subject to interpretation when it comes to sibling position. For most of our sample, their position in the sibling order as youngest, oldest or a middle child was straightforward. Overall, they were fairly evenly split between children occupying oldest, youngest and middle positions. For some, though, this position was ambiguous. An example of this is Hlynor's sibling position in his cross-national and complex family. Hlynor (age 8) had come to live in Britain with his younger brother and their shared biological parents. In this respect, he is the oldest sibling. However, Hlynor has three older half-brothers from his father's previous relationship living in his country of origin, one of whom had recently lived with them in Britain for a year. In this respect, then, Hlynor is a middle sibling. Hlynor himself describes his younger sibling as his 'real' brother, understands himself as older brother to him, and feels closer to him than he does to his other brothers. Hlynor also, however, idolises the half-brother who lived with them as older and 'cool'. It is these sorts of subjective understandings that we will be exploring in depth in this report.

Structure of the report

The report is divided into four further chapters that address key themes arising out of the children's accounts of their relationships with their brothers and sisters, followed by a final summary chapter.

Chapter 2 focuses on notions of connection and separation – on the children's feelings about being close to and caring for their siblings or being apart and autonomous from them. We look at how connection and separation are played out around particular aspects of the children's lives, notably emotions, talk and activity, possessions, and space and place, and show the importance of gender and other characteristics in the ways the children understand these everyday aspects of life with their brothers and sisters.

Chapter 3 examines the way children talk about their relationships with their brothers and sisters around the status of being the oldest, middle or youngest sibling. We show how sibling status position is more a subjective matter than it is a technical or objective fact of birth order. We look at the ideas underlying each of their discussions of birth-order status, and explore shifts in and alternatives to these, revealing that issues of power and authority are at stake.

Chapter 4 addresses past, present and future in children's understandings of the nature of their relationship with their siblings. We show how children are dealing with the changes occurring in their brothers and sisters, and themselves, over time, around age and ability, emotions, and events in their lives. Continuity can also be a feature of children's perspectives on their relationships, and this is also explored.

Chapter 5 reviews what children themselves understand as strengths and drawbacks of their relationships, with a specific focus on their coping practices in the face of any problems. We elaborate the children's oft-used term of 'annoying' to describe siblings, and detail the variety of ways in which children attempted to deal with such annoyance and more deep-rooted difficulties. We draw attention to the importance of age hierarchy, gender and so on in the children's perceptions of problems, and the coping practices that they draw on.

Finally, in Chapter 6, we draw together the main messages from our examination of children's sibling relationships in middle childhood, demonstrating their complexity and variety according to context. We then conclude by looking at the implications of our findings for practice in a variety of professional fields and initiatives.

2. Being close and being apart: connection and separation

We begin our 'insider' perspective on children's sibling relationships in middle childhood by exploring the extent to which the children who took part in this research felt close to, cared for by, and connected to their brothers and sisters, or felt apart, autonomous and separate from them. These feelings and experiences of connection and separation were played out around four recurring main themes in the children's accounts: emotions, talk and activity, possessions, and space and place. These themes are grounded in the children's own discussions of their sibling relationships. They are part of the seemingly small and taken-for-granted everyday ways that children actively 'do' or 'practise' their relationships with their brothers and sisters on expressive, material and physical levels. Some features of these themes are gendered.

Below, we address each of these four main themes in turn, but it will be evident that they also occur in interaction with one another. Further, many children moved between connection and separation in a single account. They demonstrated a mixture of understandings in relation to different aspects of their relationship with one sibling, or distinct understandings in relation to different siblings. Throughout we note that the children's attempts at connection or separation could be constrained by their siblings' own striving for the opposite.

Emotions: a sense of self

Children often talked about their siblings in ways that showed that they were an integral part of their emotional sense of who they were. They said that having brothers and sisters meant that there was always 'someone there' for them who knew them in a fundamental way. They spoke about how they loved and felt loved by their siblings, and experienced closeness and reciprocal caring for and about each other.

Having siblings gave these children emotional security and protection from an inner sense of being alone:

> I'm never really alone. But one of my friends, she doesn't have a brother or sister or a – she doesn't have anybody at all, so she misses out … Because [my sister] kind of lives with me and she shares – cos she knows more about me so I'm kind of closer to her than I would be to [friends] … I went [on a school trip for half a week] and my sister, when I got back, my sister said – I said 'Oh, did you miss me?', and she was like 'Oh yeah, it's so boring without you, I mean there's nothing to do', and I felt like really happy and stuff. So I wasn't just ignored, I wasn't not bothered about.
>
> *(Izzy, age 9, white, middle class, talking about her younger sister)*

While some children had a more individualised sense of connection (see Izzy above), others perceived themselves as belonging to a group, with their siblings providing them with a feeling of collectivity:

> They're there when I need them … My sisters help cos when they're – when I've come home and I've had a bad day at school and that, they cheer me up and they help with my homework … The best things about having sisters are they're there to help, they're around when you need them. They're there to have a good time with.
>
> *(Ellie, age 12, white, working class, talking about her co-resident older full and half sisters and her two non-resident older half sisters)*

> Brothers and sisters, they are part of your family. You love them and they love you. I help my brother, he helps me, we all help each other … Sometimes my sister helps me, she sticks up for me … Sometimes they get me presents, sometime they get me a drink if I am ill.
>
> *(Tom, age 9, white, working class, talking about his older full sister and brother)*

Relationships with siblings were not all sweetness and light, however. Nearly all the children referred to arguing and fighting with their siblings. For some, even serious disputes, as opposed to 'play fighting', were an integral part of their feeling of connection to their siblings:

> Everybody fights, every brother and sister I know fights at some time. Because if we didn't fight we'd be really, really, really weird, if we didn't fight. We'd be way out of place, we'd be just too weird. I couldn't live without fighting him.
>
> *(Claire, age 11, white, middle class, talking about her younger full brother)*

For other children, however, arguments and fights felt more like points of division, existing alongside the inner sense of a connected self:

> [My brother and sisters] are closer to me [than friends] because they're like family … I've lived with my family longer obviously, so I know them better than I know my friends … [Brothers and sisters] quite often look after each other, but quite often they start fights … [The worst thing is] we don't always like the same thing and the slightest argument always starts a fight.
>
> *(Jason, age 11, white, working class, talking about his older full sister and younger full brother)*

Not all the children taking part in the research had feelings of connection, caring and closeness to their siblings. Some children in particular had a strong sense of self as apart and separate, regarding their brothers and sisters as violating their autonomy. They intensely disliked their siblings being around:

> I don't really like them … I spend most of the time by myself. And then they come up [to the bedroom] and destroy it, destroy the thing that I've been playing with. Especially [my brother] because it's his bedroom as well … They are going to come to my school and I don't want them to … I'm going to be fast away from them [when they come]. I'm like – I am faster [at running], I'm the second fastest in my class.
>
> *(Jacob, age 8, white, middle class, talking about his younger full sister and two younger full brothers)*

Overall, however, most of the children felt a positive emotional connection to their brothers and sisters, alongside everyday disputes that meant that they wanted to be apart and separate from them at times. Issues of being close or apart were further played out around the other main themes in the children's accounts.

Talk and activity

Talking and doing activities together were recurrent and tangible features of the children's connection to, or separation from, their siblings. They were also largely gendered practices. For the most part, talking together was presented by girls as a significant aspect of their connection to their sisters. In contrast, doing activities together was regarded by boys as a significant aspect of connection between brothers. Furthermore, in the case of brother–sister relationships, it appeared that

Figure 2.1 Jacob's drawing of his sister lying
on the floor because he punched her

activities largely took precedence over talk as a feature of connection. In other words, the relationship worked on male terms, revealing gendered power relations.

These points are well illustrated by children who had both brothers and sisters. Anne (age 11) was a white working-class girl who lived with her older full brother, Jay (age 18), and their mother, in a large city. She had an older full sister, Natasha (age 21), who had recently moved away to another part of the country. Anne's relationship with Natasha was, to a large extent, characterised by talk, which was the case even before she left home, while her relationship with Jay was spoken about in terms of shared – or prevented – activities:

> [An older sister] is someone to help you, someone to help you with your homework, someone to talk to, someone to look after you and be kind to you ... I spend a lot of time with my sister when I go and see her with my mum. [We] just talk about life ... [If I was upset] I would go to my sister ... Cos my sister has moved, like I keep in contact with her and like that makes me feel better cos I still know what she looks like and what her voice sounds like and things like that. We write letters, we, um, talk to each other on the phone and we send text messages to each other ... My brother's got a drum kit now. He don't let me [play on it]. I went 'Jay, can I sit at your drum kit?', and he goes 'No!', and I goes 'Oh why?', [and he replied] 'Cos I don't want you breaking nothing', and so I'm like 'Owwh' ... But sometimes I spend time with my brother. Like sometimes he takes me to the cinema to see different films, but not all the time ... We do get on with each other. But sometimes we muck around and beat each other up, but not hurt each other, but just muck about ... Well, he does let me watch his DVDs ... He helps me with my homework if I get stuck on it.

Daniel (age 9) and his sister Sapphire (age 8) were interviewed together. They were white, working class, and lived in a village with their mother and step-father, older half sister and younger full sister. They also had a non-resident older half brother. Daniel understood shared play activities in gendered terms, although Sapphire seemed to do her best to go along with his preferences:

Daniel: Well, I play gun games with Sapphire and we play in the centre, we play games, erm, play on the slides, play in the garden ... It is a bit boring. Like there is no one to play with who is boys, play football and stuff. I asked [my older sister], she did used to. Like she kicked it and then she just said 'Oh it's boooring' and just went in. But like if there was another boy, we would play more, like with cars and stuff ... [My older brother] used to, though, play football. Now he stays in and watches whatever my dad does [on TV] ...

Sapphire: [Daniel] likes shooting games. I like shooting too. We go shooting round the house.

For boys, a lack of shared activities with brothers and sisters (as for Daniel with his older sister and brother above) and, for girls, an inability to talk and confide in sisters often represented a sense of complete or partial separation in the relationship:

It depends on what mood she's in. If she's in like a stressy mood, she'll just talk about the room and stuff. And if she's in a really stressful mood, she'll tell me to go away. And then if she's like in a really good mood and she's like going out somewhere, we'll talk about boys and stuff ... I sort of wish she'd be here a bit more, but, yeah, cos if she was here, I'd like – she'd probably be like a bit closer, but she's not so I don't really talk to her. When I was in junior school, it was like really – it was like my sister was my best friend, but now, er, she's like doing stuff and I'm stuck at home.
(Natalie, age 12, white, working class, talking about her older full sister)

Of course, brothers did refer to talking to each other and sisters did undertake activities together. Indeed, several girls explained elaborate fantasy role games that they played with their sisters. For the most part, though, shared activities between sisters, or talk between brothers or brother and sister, were not stressed as a core aspect of the relationship. Two working-class boys were the exceptions to this gendered dimension to sibling relationships. One of these was Bob (age 8), of Pakistani origin, who lived in a nuclear family in a city. Bob had a strong sense of being the oldest brother to his three younger full brothers (age 7, 5 and 3) and spent a lot of time talking to them in an authoritative and paternal role:

> I like teaching them things because it's quite fun ... I ask the teachers every day how's their behaviours, how their behaviour's been, and then if it's bad, when they come home, I don't hit them, I just tell them off, I just shout at them ... When they were babies, I always had to play baby games with them, I had to talk baby talk with them. And now they're older I can talk properly with them.

The other exception was Eddie (age 10), a white, working-class boy, who lived in a step-family, in a village, with his younger half sister, China (age 8). In talking about his relationship with China, in addition to shared activities, he stressed the importance of confiding in each other:

> We can play with each other, we can talk to each other about things ... We can talk about our problems ... Like when I argue with my friends in school I tell her. I know I can trust her ... [We also talk about] like the best songs and TV programmes and stuff like that. What we like and what we don't like, our work at school, projects we are on and how to improve our things on the computer and stuff like that.

China appeared to wield more power in their relationship, for example taking charge of the TV remote control and deciding which programmes they watched. China was also interviewed for this study and she stressed that Eddie had a different biological father who lived elsewhere, while Eddie did not mention this. It may have been that – unlike other children in similar situations in our research – Eddie had to work hard to feel part of a collective unit with his sister and had to adopt a more unusual gendered method to do so.

Possessions

Possessions, such as games, toys, books, clothes and so on, were another main theme that could demonstrate the extent of closeness or division between the children and their siblings. For some, sharing or jointly owning possessions, or receiving gifts from their brothers and sisters, were aspects of connection:

> They give me money. Like whenever I need it they give it to me really ... I let them in my bedroom, I let them go on my Playstation[2] ...
>
> *Interviewer:* How do you work out all your stuff, sharing and that?
>
> I just get all my stuff on one side [of the shared bedroom] and put all his stuff on that side. He can use my stuff and I use his.
> *(Lee, age 10, white, working class, talking about his two older full brothers, one of whom shares his bedroom)*

For other children, disputes about who has priority over, or ownership of, possessions, and distinctions between the sorts of possessions each sibling had, were symbols of separation:

> And she goes through all my magazines when I tell her not to. I don't like it but she still goes through them. Cos she gets children's magazines but I get big ones ... Once I walked in on her putting my make-up on and I don't like it ... She only has lip gloss and nail varnish but I have eye liner, lip gloss, lipstick, everything. I've got tattoos, fake ones. So I get them and she puts them on, and I just get really, really, really annoyed with it. Cos like she takes my clothes, like she goes out in my coats when I tell her not to. She tries to wear my shoes out, she tries to wear my make-up.
> *(Mariko, age 9, white, middle class, talking about her younger full sister)*

An interweaving of sharing and disputes around possessions was evident in most of the children's accounts. Some children experienced a sense of separation from their siblings through distinct ownership of possessions, whereas for other children sharing possessions with their siblings seemed unremarkable.

Space and place

The children's feelings of being close to or apart from their siblings were played out in different spaces and places – the home and different rooms within it, especially bedrooms, and outside the home, at school and in the neighbourhood. Some children also had full, half or step-siblings living in a different household, sometimes

---

2   Olivia says: 'A Playstation is a sort of game that you can play on telly. You plug it into the telly in a special way. You choose the game you want to play and then you put the game in and you start playing. The game is on a disk. You can have all different sorts of games. You've got a special remote hand control and you press the buttons to do things that you want to do.'

in another part of the UK or another country altogether, and their feelings of connection or separation were set within this geographical backdrop.

Within the home, children's access to bedroom space in relation to their siblings was an issue. Some children, especially those with a number of siblings, seemed to share quite cramped houses and bedroom space without much rancour. Callum (age 12), a white, working-class boy, for example, lived in a step-family in a large city with his older full brother, a younger full brother, and younger half brother and sister. He talked about sharing a bedroom with all his siblings without mentioning any conflict:

> [There are] two bunkbeds and another bed at the bottom of the bunkbed.
>
> *Interviewer:* So how do you work out where everybody's stuff goes?
>
> We've got drawers under the beds, we've got that. Big drawers under the bed where all the toys go and that. We share wardrobes.

Generally, however, girls felt that they needed some privacy, when they were changing their clothes in particular. Other children seemed to be preoccupied more with conflict over shared bedroom space even where they had large rooms, and experienced having their own space as a crucial part of their autonomy:

> I have got my own room. Yeah and [my brother and sister] share a room, and my mum and dad share a room, and I have a room to myself. I love it … I write a note, I say that – I put a note on the outside of my bedroom door saying no one allowed in my room … I hated it when I shared with [my brother] and now I am really glad I got my own room cos it stays tidy most of the time.
> *(Harry Potter, age 9, white, middle class, talking about his younger full brother and sister)*

Caring, or alternatively dissociated, relationships at home could be carried over into places outside, at school and/or in the neighbourhood. Kelly (age 10) was middle class and of black African/white British parentage, living in a small city. As well as two older full sisters, she had a younger full sister and brother, and her cousin and his mother also lived with them. Her account was dominated by caring connections within the home and a protective watchfulness outside of it by herself and the other siblings. There may well be concern about racism here, although Kelly did not refer to this as the issue:

> Like when there is a bully in school and [my younger sister] – and my brother and my sister, they just pick on them. Well, there is this boy, this

was in year three with [my sister], and he was chasing her around the playground. So [she] came to me and I started chasing him around the playground, and then I caught him and took him to the teacher. Because I am pretty fast ... My little brother used to [look after me when I was bullied] as well.

In distinction to carrying over a relationship across places, children sometimes talked about having a different sort of relationship with their brothers and sisters outside the home, at school and/or in the neighbourhood, from that inside it. For example, they could experience more connection with their siblings in the home and more separation at school or play space outside the home, or vice versa. This could also change around particular issues, for example experiencing dissociation from a sibling at school or within the neighbourhood generally, but connection and support if bullying occurs there. These shifting relationships in different places can be quite complex.

Callum's (quoted above) younger full brother Jake (age 9) was also interviewed, separately, for this research. Both of their accounts demonstrate an intricate inter-weaving of several issues. In each, there is a taken-for-granted closeness within the home (and as discussed earlier, five siblings shared a bedroom). This is cross-cut with wanting separation – at school and playing out in the woods – from younger brother/s (in Callum's case, including Jake). Each also has a thwarted connection with their older brother/s (in Jake's case, including Callum). For example, Jake explained:

> [At home] I watch videos with [my younger siblings] ... [We all play] on the Playstation, hide and seek and everything like that ...[When Callum was at the same school as me] sometimes we used to play football together ... It's annoying [having my younger brother at my school] because when I'm playing football he always comes over to me and asks me questions ... [And] when I'm down the shops with mum and want to go into the sweet shop [my younger brother] always wants to come with [me]. I shout at him and say no, no ... I ask [Callum] to come with me [to play in the woods] and he don't so I have to go up there on my own and that.

In contrast, Bethany (age 9), a white, working-class girl who lived in a nuclear family in a city, described a conflict-based relationship with her older full brother (age 15) inside the home, which she understood in gendered terms. At school and in the neighbourhood, however, she spoke of him as more caring and protective:

> He did used to go to my school with me. [It was] nice because he used to stick up for me against the bullies. Like if they were calling me names he

would ask them to stop ... Sometimes he does stick up for me if I am crying, like when we are out on the street ... [At home] he's annoying. He beats me up and chucks me down on the sofa. One time we were playing on the computer and I went to get a drink of water and he just chucked it down me. It went all over me ... I think all brothers are like that. Most of them. Cos my friend's brothers aren't nice.

Place, in terms of different locations, was an issue for children who had siblings who did not live with them, with some far away. Sometimes, 'visiting' sibship meant that children felt that they did not know their siblings very well:

We only go and see [our step-siblings] every holiday ... I don't really get to see them that much. And I know [my full sister], and [my step-siblings] I just don't know them that much, you know. I know them, I just don't know them that much. I mean, I can't really trust them [not to betray confidences] ... I feel [some responsibility towards them as an older sister] as well a bit. But it isn't really the same [as for my full sister] because they're all the way in [city].
(*Laura, age 10, white, middle class, talking about her non-resident younger step-sister and step-brother, and her co-resident younger full sister*)

Other children felt a closeness over geographical distance, as we saw for Anne with her older sister, in the 'Talk and activity' section. One boy wanted 'visiting' sibship to become co-residential to enhance connection, while another moved between different households with different siblings in each, appreciating the sense of separation:

[My sister] is always backwards and forwards [between houses] all the time ... [I would like to go to the same school as her] cos then [she] can live in one place and I don't have to take a trip to go and see her ... [If we went to the same school] I'd play football with her.
(*Fred, age 11, white, working class, talking about his non-resident half sister*)

When I come here on Fridays [for the weekend] then I think oh there's always a break from my brother and sisters ... [And when I leave my sisters here to go back to my other home and siblings] I'm happy. I'm used to [leaving them] so I'm not really bothered.
(*Michael, age 10, Asian, middle class, talking about the two younger half siblings he lives with at weekends and the three younger half siblings he lives with during the week*)

Clearly, looking at space and place, including residential location, introduces a number of complexities into sibling relationships. Nonetheless, these are also demonstrations of underlying issues of connection and separation that are evident in the other key themes that we have already examined.

Conclusion

In this chapter we have seen that, for many children, their brothers and sisters were an integral part of their sense of who they were, offering them emotional connection, care and protection against inner loneliness, at the same time as there were points of division around arguments over possessions, bedroom space and so on. Feelings of closeness or separation in relationships with siblings at home were either carried over into relationships with them at school or the neighbourhood, or children experienced a different sort of relationship with their brothers and sisters outside the home from that within it. There were, however, some gender aspects to feeling both connected and apart from siblings.

Gender was a particularly relevant issue in whether children stressed talk and confiding in each other, or shared activities, in their relationship with their siblings. Talking together was often presented by girls as an important part of their connection to their sisters, while boys usually regarded doing activities together as demonstrating closeness to their brothers. Brother–sister relationships revealed gendered power relations, with activities largely taking precedence over talk. Girls felt that an inability to talk to and confide in their sisters represented a sense of separation in their relationship, while boys regarded a lack of shared activities with their siblings similarly.

There were also differences in children's sense of a self who was connected to or separate from their brothers and sisters, and the aspects of everyday life that they regarded as important in this. Some children felt that their siblings provided them with a feeling of being part of a collective group. In some cases, they also seemed to see sharing and joint ownership of possessions as unremarkable. In addition, some children talked about sharing quite limited bedroom space with siblings without mentioning any conflict. In contrast, other children had a strong sense of self as apart and separate from their brothers and sisters. They felt that their siblings violated their autonomy, and were concerned with establishing ownership of distinct possessions rather than sharing them. Having their own bedroom was also regarded by some children as a crucial part of their autonomy and separation from their siblings.

Status distinctions between siblings, as younger or older, were evident in some of the material we have presented in this chapter as well. This topic is a preoccupation of much literature and previous research on siblings (see Chapter 1), and we look at it from children's own point of view in the next chapter.

3. Being the oldest, youngest or middle sibling

In this chapter we explore children's ways of talking about their relationships with their brothers and sisters in terms of the status of being the oldest, youngest or middle sibling. As we noted in Chapter 1, research addressing children's sibling status, such as birth-order studies, often treats this as unproblematic. Children's positions in the status hierarchy are regarded as objective, ascribed and technical facts. In other words, this work takes being oldest, middle or youngest child as biologically fixed – determined by the birth order within a family and not by children's own understandings and interactions. In contrast, in this chapter we demonstrate that children's experiences of their status position in the sibling order are subjective, complex and context specific. That is to say that children create their own understanding of their sibling position in interaction with their brothers and sisters within the particular circumstances of their lives.

Sibling status order can be particularly fluid in complex families, and we begin by looking at this issue, before turning to examine the ideas associated with being an older and a younger brother or sister, and with being a middle sibling. Matters of power and authority are at stake in the ways that children talk about sibling position, and these can be subject to transformation. Shifts in power and authority in particular contexts play their part in calling the sibling hierarchy into question, and discussion of this forms the focus of the last part of this chapter.

Sibling status in complex family living arrangements

In Chapter 1 we argued that, given the complexities of family life, the 'facts' of sibling status order can be subject to interpretation by researchers, and demonstrated this by considering the question of Hlynor's shifting sibling position in his cross-national family. Sibling position is also subject to interpretation by children themselves. It is apparent that, for children living in complex family and household arrangements, there can be ambiguities in defining which status position they occupy. This is particularly the case for children with siblings who live elsewhere and who have infrequent or no contact. Further, in cases where children have an older sibling living outside their household with whom they do have contact, they often understand themselves to be an older sibling in relation to the younger siblings they live with. Moreover, children can see other children, who are part of their family but who are not biologically related to them, as siblings.

Thomas's (age 10) situation illustrates the complexities both of family life and of children's understandings of sibling position. He was a white, working-class boy, living in a village with his mother. He had an older step-brother, Rick (age 19), who lived in a distant town and sometimes visited, but was due to return to the home more permanently in the future. Within this relationship, Thomas positioned himself as a younger sibling. His father lived in a city some distance away with his partner and her two daughters: Saffron (age 8) and Emmelia (age 9). Thomas referred to Saffron and Emmelia as his younger 'sisters', hence positioning himself as older brother when he visited them. Thomas's account of his sibling relationships revealed marked shifts in his status position associated with both Rick's and his own coming and goings. When Rick came home, Thomas was the younger brother, and when Thomas visited his father, he became the older brother:

Thomas:	I'm not exactly the youngest, second youngest.
Interviewer:	So you're more like the middle one?
Thomas:	Yeah.
Interviewer:	And what's it like being the middle one?
Thomas:	Horrible, cos when I'm up here [with my mother] I don't have to do a thing but when I go up there it's like I have to do everything! … It's fun but I hate doing stuff for Saffron and Emmelia all the time …
Interviewer:	Do you look after Rick?
Thomas:	No, you have to be older than them to look after them.

The flexibility of Thomas's status position is heightened by the fact that, for the majority of the time, he lived almost as an only child with his mother. His account demonstrates the complex nature of some children's relationships with their brothers and sisters where they may not all live together. It also heralds several of the issues that we discuss in the rest of this chapter, particularly relating to ideas about being older and younger, and how middle siblings understand their position.

Ideas about being older or being younger

The ideas underlying the children's ways of talking about being older or younger than their brothers and sisters involve issues of power and authority. Many children referred to older siblings as exercising care and protection over younger brothers and sisters, and younger siblings as receivers of this safekeeping:

> My older brother and sister stick up for me ... around the house and in the street ... My little brother goes to the same school as me and we have to go there on the bus, so I help him on the bus.
> *(Emily, age 11, white, middle class, talking about her younger full brother, age 5)*

> When [my brother] was a little baby and my mum was in the shower, he would suck my finger when he was crying. When he needed a nappy change when it was just a wee, I would change it for him ... I taught [my sister] to walk ... I showed her one night.
> *(Mariko, age 9, talking about her younger full sister, age 6, and brother, age 4)*

Children talked about the usefulness of older brothers and sisters in protecting younger siblings from being bullied at school or on the street. Bart (age 12) and his brother Zack (age 9) were interviewed together. They lived in a small city, in a nuclear, white, middle-class family. Bart characterised his relationship with Zack as one of 'best friendship'. Both boys, however, had distinct ideas about being older and younger brothers, and this centred largely around protection, caring and responsibility:

Zack:	He's in secondary school now and I'm in primary school. It was good [when we were in the same school] because if someone was picking on me I could go and tell my brother and he would come and sort it out for me.
Bart:	I don't go to the same school as my brother but I want to so if he gets into any trouble I can stick up for him. Yeah, people down the street keep kicking his bike and he got a stone thrown at him at school but we didn't know who it was so I couldn't do anything about it ...
Interviewer:	And did Zack ever help you and stick up for you [Bart]?
Zack:	It's mainly older brothers that stick up for younger brothers.

On occasions, some older siblings allied themselves further up the family status hierarchy, with parents. This was particularly notable in Bob's case. As we saw in Chapter 2, Bob's identity as the oldest brother within his family was strongly linked to a type of paternal authority based on care, protection and hierarchy, involving systems of sanctions and rewards:

> My dad sometimes brings us sweets, and I sometimes give some of my, some of the sweets to my brothers, if they've been good in school. You know, my father, since I'm the oldest, he's older than me, he teaches me things so then I can be the cleverest in my class. Like, d'you know, like lessons, home lessons, like we do in school, like Maths and English and things. It's the same with me, I think, cos in the future when I'm older, I'm gonna, I'm gonna help them with their things as well, so they can be the cleverest in the class and can get a good job … a good future.
> *(Bob, age 9, Asian, working class, talking about his three younger brothers)*

Bob's focus on helping his younger brothers with their schoolwork echoes many children's stress on older siblings acting as knowledgeable role models generally, including helping younger ones with their homework:

> [My brother] helps me through with my homework if I get stuck on it … Cos like if your older brothers or sisters are at college or university and you're at secondary school or primary school, then they can help you because they have been through it.
> *(Anne, age 11, white, working class, talking about her co-resident older full brother, age 18)*

> [My sister] is very interesting, intelligent, helps me if I am stuck with homework.
> *(Sam, age 11, white, middle class, talking about his non-resident older half sister, age 19)*

Being a middle sibling

Children who were middle brothers or sisters drew on ideas about both older and younger status in shifting ways, rather than having a distinct way of talking about being a middle sibling. Chris (age 11) provides a good example. He lived in a white, middle-class nuclear family in a city with his older brother, Robert (age 16), younger sister, Abbey (age 9), and younger brother, Jack (age 6). Chris's account contained elements of both older and younger sibling positions (in much the same way as for Thomas and Emily, each quoted earlier in this chapter). Chris's discussion of the strengths and weaknesses of having brothers and sisters illustrates how he shifted between younger and older ideas to understand his middle position:

Chris: The best things are, [brothers and sisters] are fun to play with, they help you with your homework and they also, well Robert helps with the computer if something goes wrong. The worse things are, they interfere with things, older brothers and sisters look down on you. Like Robert, he like is older so he thinks he knows more, well he does but you know it's like (sighs). When I don't know things, he makes it like I don't know that much. If he like knows more things than you it's really, um ...

Interviewer: [pointing to Chris's list of the worst things about brothers and sisters] So what do you mean interfering?

Chris: Well, Jack, like cos I share a bedroom with him, if I have friends over he starts like coming in and interfering with us. It is all right when I don't have friends round but when I do, it is annoying.

As with other children in his position, throughout Chris's account there was no distinct discussion of being a 'middle' sibling. Rather, he understood his position in the birth order as made up of being younger in relation to his older brother and being older in relation to his younger brother and sister, using the same ideas as children who were the oldest and youngest sibling in their family.

Transformations to older and younger status positioning

While many children adhered to the ideas associated with their position in the birth order, it is also the case that older and younger status positions were called into question in some of their accounts. These had the potential to transform notions of ascribed birth order positions in the sibling status hierarchy. For the most part contingent, they occurred at moments or in a more sustained form, in several main ways:

- when older brothers or sisters were in need of care and protection, and the younger sibling took on the role of meeting these needs, thus reversing the dominant idea of older siblings as givers of care or protection and younger siblings as receivers;
- when children drew on other ideas associated with gendered identities, as feminine or masculine; and
- when younger siblings posed their older brother or sister as failing to adhere to the ideas associated with being older and saw them as acting in ways more associated with being younger.

These bases for transformations to older and younger status positioning can cross-cut. We discuss each of them in turn, drawing attention to where they interact.

Care and protection

Reversals of the ideas about giving care associated with being an older sibling often occurred in the children's accounts when they spoke about younger brothers and sisters looking after their older sibling, which was especially appreciated when they were ill:

> Like she gets all my clothes out for like when I want to go and play, and she says I want to choose. And she puts my hair up sometimes, even though it does fall out after about five minutes. And, erm, when I am ill she gets me a blanket and puts it on me. When I am asleep in the living room she cuddles up to me.
>
> *(Mariko, age 9, white, middle class, talking about her younger sister, age 6)*

Younger siblings sometimes also called into question their ascribed status position when their older brother or sister was in need of care and protection, and this was particularly the case outside the home, on the street and at school. Younger siblings could help their older brothers and sisters at times of bullying by offering support and advice. Richard (age 12) lived with his mother, step-father and half sister, Elsa (age 4). The family were white and middle class, and lived in a large city. Richard explained how he coped with being bullied at school:

> I might talk to [my step-father] or Elsa. Sometimes Elsa comes up with ideas that sound amusing that make me feel better. Like if someone hurt me at school then she would say, 'Well you could hurt them back or you could tell the teacher or you could tell yourself that someone hits you.'

She thinks that if you tell yourself you will be able to get rid of it and take it off. Make it better ... Well it doesn't [make it better], she just thinks that it does ... When somebody hurt me at school and she was worried, [she] said, 'What's the matter?' And I said, 'Something is happening at school' and she said, 'You can take it [the horrible feeling] off as if it is a sticker' ... It made me feel better because she always seems to see the funny side of it.

Richard confiding in Elsa, and her attempts at comforting her brother and helping him deal with bullying, can be seen as a reversal of the conventional sibling status order of older care-giver and younger receiver.

Another example is provided by Kelly (age 10) and her sister, Jessie (age 8), who were of black African and white parentage, and lived in a middle-class extended family containing their own parents and older and younger siblings, and their cousin and his mother. In Chapter 2 we noted that Kelly talked a great deal about how she and her siblings exercised a protective watchfulness over each other outside the home. Kelly and Jessie together described how their youngest brother, Mark (age 6), was able to stick up for Jessie:

Kelly:	[My siblings] look after me, they help me with stuff I don't understand like my Mum and Dad do, and they look after me when I get bullied as well. My friends did and my brother. Like my little brother Mark used to do that as well. Once when Jessie, yeah, this boy in her class kept kicking her, and Mark, yeah, said 'Leave my sister alone' ...
Jessie:	Yep, tell her about the party and the balloon stick.
Kelly:	When my brother went to [a friend's] party with Jessie he went straight with the balloon stick [to a boy who bullied Jessie at school] and hit him with it.

Kelly and Jessie's accounts (along with those of their cousin Edward, who was also interviewed) focused on shared memories of living in Africa and their activity centred around these past experiences. This feeling of togetherness in a new country, and the apparent threat of bullies, may account for the reversal in status positioning for their younger brother. It may also demonstrate a gendered dimension, with a brother protecting a sister even if he is younger than her. It is to ideas about femininity and masculinity as enabling shifts in status order that we now turn.

Femininity and masculinity

Children were able to draw on ideas associated with gendered identities, as feminine or masculine, in various ways to achieve shifts of their position at particular moments or in more sustained ways. Some children talked about the imaginary games that they played with their siblings, which could reverse the birth-order status. Laura (age 10) and Jasmine (age 7) were full sisters who were interviewed together. They lived in a white middle-class step-family in a small rural village. The sisters played fantasy games in which Jasmine appeared to set out to differentiate herself from her older sister through the roles that they played, with a complex interplay between power and gender:

Jasmine:	I normally play the Princess. Laura likes to play all the different characters.
Interviewer:	What characters have you been then Laura?
Laura:	Oh well, in Cinderella, I've been the Prince, the Fairy Godmother, the…
Jasmine:	… Evil Queen.
Laura:	There is no Evil Queen. The Prince, the Fairy Godmother, and that's about it.
Jasmine:	The Ugly Sister.
Interviewer:	What was your best character then, Laura, do you think? Your best performance? Which one did you enjoy being?
Jasmine:	I think 'Princess and the Pea' is the goodest one, because there's always laughing in it and there's only three people so you don't need three people to play, and of course, I was the Princess, and I was the King and the Queen.
Laura:	The Queen and the Prince. Actually, I was the caretaker.
Jasmine:	We made up the caretaker.

In this interaction, Jasmine explicitly asserted herself over Laura, almost like an older sister even though she was three years younger. Moreover, it was Jasmine who chose to act out the popular, powerful and successful characters from traditional fairytales. When Laura tried to tell the interviewer about the characters she has played, Jasmine interrupted, reminding her of her less glamorous, subservient or evil roles.

Underpinning the sisters' play are gendered ideas associated with femininity and power. Laura accepted her less glamorous roles and the corresponding associations, and both sisters understood them as related to her own personality traits:

Jasmine:	[Laura] doesn't really like to be the Princess.
Laura:	I'm just not that kind of girl, I don't really like being the Princess in the top rank, I just like things the way they are. I mean, if I was a Princess, I'd never be able to walk.

In stark contrast, Jasmine established herself as generally more feminine, pretty and popular, than Laura, although Laura attempted to resist this:

Jasmine:	Laura's a bit fatter, Laura's a bit chubbier.
Laura:	You're chubby, you're chubby.
Jasmine:	Laura's not a dressy skirt person. She wants to but first she's got to get rid of her chubby body … Our hairs are different. Mine's a bit longer … I've got friends and she hasn't. She used to have this friend called Mary.
Laura:	Well actually she still is.

Figure 3.1 Jasmine's drawing of the fantasy fairytale
games she plays with her older sister, Laura

Gendered shifts in the sibling status order could also be precipitated by parents, rather than being actively initiated by the children themselves. In Chapter 2, we discussed Eddie's (age 10) possible vested interest in maintaining a feeling of being part of a collective unit with his younger half sister, China (age 8). In their joint account, Eddie emphasised his desire for equality, negotiation and fairness as opposed to control over his sister. In their family it was the youngest sibling, China, who was able to take up a more powerful position in the shared activity of watching television, drawing on a notion of strength associated with masculinity. Both children agreed that this decision had been made by their father (Eddie's step-father) because he regarded Eddie as too rough with the remote control, while China was seen as more gentle. The result was that Eddie was subject to China's authority; he had to ask her permission when he wanted to watch programmes on another channel – although, as a girl, China was left out of some activities as not being strong enough:

Eddie:	Yeah, but she gets to handle the control and I don't. She gets to change the channel … It's just China who decides [what programmes to watch]. Sometimes I can ask to put programmes on … Because my father won't let me use it.
China:	Because he presses it too hard. The last time the button came off. So Daddy put a ban on him.
Eddie:	[It makes me feel] angry, I think it should be that I get to use the control every so often and she gets it every so often to make it fair …
China:	Daddy comes with us [to play tennis], but one time they went out and played together but I was left on my own because I am a girl … They think I can't hit the ball but sometimes I can, but Eddie hits it too hard.

Eddie's preference for fairness and equality in itself calls into question the sibling-order hierarchy – an alternative to the reversal of the status order created by his step-father's intervention. We look at this sort of suspension of sibling positioning later. Next we examine transformations around age status.

Failure to adhere to being older

Some children shifted sibling status positioning by posing their older brother or sister as failing to adhere to the qualities associated with being an older sibling, replacing them with attributes that are associated with being the younger sibling.

This then – explicitly or implicitly – allowed the younger sibling to give themselves characteristics that are part of the older, more powerful and superior status. This transformation was the case for Cora (age 13) who lived in a white, working-class, nuclear family with her older brother, Gordon (age 16). Cora called into question her status as younger sister by criticising Gordon's lack of maturity for his age in a way that drew on gendered ideas about teenage masculinity. She believed that they could build a more positive relationship if Gordon acted in ways that were consistent with his older, teenage male status. By positioning her brother as immature, Cora was able to place herself as more 'grown up':

> He is just immature. Because he doesn't act like older ... [Friends with older brothers and sisters] get on probably better than younger brothers and sisters. Cos they, they're more mature and, I don't know really. I just think, cos they're older ... Maybe if he went out more ... Cos I'm probably more grown up than he is. I wish he'd go out more and act more like a teenager. Cos like, most folk go out and hang about, and then if he went and did that I think he'd grow up more. Cos I've sort of grown up more faster than him. I wish he'd just hang out with his friends cos maybe he'd start to grow up.

The means of calling into question the ideas associated with the dominant sibling birth-order status do not really set aside the notion of characteristics associated with sibling position. Rather, they are created in particular moments when the older sibling is in need of supportive care and protection, or fails to adhere to the ideas associated with being older, or draw on another set of ideas that impose a different sort of sibling division based on masculinity or femininity. Whatever the means, status divisions and power imbalances are still apparent. A more serious suspension of notions of hierarchy and power, however, was evident in some of the children's accounts, where there was a partial or total absence of sibling status position.

The absence of sibling status position

Some children drew on notions of equality and fairness instead of birth-order hierarchy to understand and talk about their sibling relationships. Rachel (age 9) lived in a white, working-class, nuclear family with her younger brother, Toby (age 7), in a small town. Unlike many other children, Rachel did not focus on the status difference between herself and her brother, although gender differences are prominent in her account. Rather, in her discussion of getting into rows with parents and the distribution of housework, there was an emphasis on fairness and sharing that rendered the birth-order hierarchy immaterial:

> Because me and Toby both get treated the same, we don't – I like better being the older because if I get a row for doing something and Toby did it as well, he'd get a row as well so we'd both get, yeah, we both have, like maybe cos – in the summer we still have mud around the house, around the place, and muddy feet prints all over the floor, so we got into trouble for that ... Well I sometimes help Mum and Dad cook, we make chips and all that, er, I sometimes help hoover, and things like dust and wash, er, that sort of thing. We split the house in half, like [Toby] gets that side of the house and I get to do like the living room and things ... Well we sometimes do it at the same time and different times, so, mm, I think it's equal. It doesn't really bother me [being the older sister].

Rachel seemed to attribute her sense of equality between herself and her brother – as opposed to a hierarchical relationship of older sister and younger brother – to the way that her parents treat them. This sense of fairness, sharing and equality between the siblings means that Rachel did not feel burdened by the responsibilities associated with being the older sibling, nor did she seem to miss the power that is also associated with it.

Conclusion

We started this chapter by showing how sibling position is not a straightforward matter when children are living in complex family and household arrangements. In these situations, children's technical status as oldest, middle or youngest brother or sister in a sibling group, and their perception of their position, can shift according to setting. Nonetheless, we also demonstrated how many older and younger siblings' understandings did adhere to notions of ascribed and fixed birth-order positions. The children's discussions highlighted underlying ideas about being either older or younger as involving issues of power and authority. Older siblings had it, while younger siblings were subject to it. Moreover, middle siblings also drew on these ideas to understand their position. They talked about being both older and younger in shifting ways, rather than having a specific way to talk about being a middle brother or sister.

Nonetheless, there are cases of transformations in, or an alternative to, sibling position in children's accounts. We explored the ways in which status hierarchy can be called into question at particular moments, around care and protection. Gendered ideas also provided a means of shifting status position for children, as did young siblings' perceptions of older brothers' or sisters' lack of adherence to the ideas associated with their place in the birth order. Again, these transformations involve issues of hierarchy and power. For some children, however, the association between sibling status position and power was muted in, and sometimes completely absent from, their accounts of their relationships with their brothers and sisters. Instead, they focused on equality and fairness in characterising older and younger sibling relationships.

Our discussion of the varying and complex ways in which children understand being the oldest, middle or youngest sibling raises issues of change in children's relationships with their brothers and sisters. We turn to examine this in more detail in the next chapter.

4. Change and continuity

This chapter explores children's understandings of the past, present and future, and change in their relationships with their brothers and sisters. Change and transition in children's lives is often regarded as a problem in policy and practice, such as through divorce (Edwards 2002). Yet, here we show that children are experiencing change as an everyday part of their sibling relationships.

Children's awareness of changes that occur over time in themselves and in brothers and sisters provides a social context for the themes addressed in the previous chapters. Clearly these previous themes are not static: feelings of connection and separation, and perceptions of sibling status all unfold over time. This attention to the passage of time further challenges a view of sibling ties as fixed and universal.

The focus here is on how children make sense of change and continuity over time in connections and separations between themselves and their brothers and sisters around their own and their siblings' age and abilities, sometimes drawing on developmental ideas concerning growing ability and competence. Other examples of change over time include memories of significant events such as the birth of a younger sibling or an older sibling leaving home, which then alters the relationship. Children can also understand change as momentary and happening in the present, for example as they or brothers and sisters experience different moods.

There are a few exceptions to this, however, where children do not envisage change in sibling relationships, either from the past to the present or from the present into the future. Continuity of relationships over time can also be a feature of children's feelings of closeness to, or autonomy from, their brothers and sisters.

Age-related competence

Some children described how their relationship had changed as their younger brothers and sisters became more competent over time. In Chapter 3 we saw how some children associated becoming older with acquiring greater competence. This notion is linked to a developmental sense of age. Some children referred to their younger siblings as less competent and restricted in their abilities. Holly (age 9), for example, lived in a white, middle-class, nuclear family in a large city with her younger sister, Jessica (age 5). She described the limitations that age placed on the domestic tasks that Jessica could carry out:

> She's too young to lay the table as she normally just sets all the things in the wrong place, even though sometimes if she's really careful she can do it properly. She can't really dust as she's not tall enough, and she can't really do the washing up as her hands don't reach into the basin and she might get cut by the knives. She can't look after me because I'm older than her and that's it, she just can't really do them. It's an age thing.

Michael (age 10) was of Pakistani origin, and the oldest brother in both of the middle-class households that he lived in, in a city. He moved between living with his father, step-mother and two younger half siblings during the week, and with his mother, step-father and three younger half siblings at weekends. Michael had noticed that one of his younger brothers, Kashif (age 3), had become less compliant:

> [Kashif] probably started changing when he was about one year old because he was really good first and he always used to do whatever you told him. But then, once he was running around the room and there was a table in front of him and he fell and he split all his nose open. And then, since that, he's been really naughty.

With five younger siblings, Michael felt that the older and more competent they grew, the less malleable they became. Moving between two households, he was well placed to observe changes in others over time. The dual household arrangement was a change that he said he initiated himself (previously living with his mother during the week and visiting his father at weekends), which meant that he had also chosen to 'swap' weekly living with one sibling group for the other group.

Other children remembered clearly the moment when age made a difference to displays of physical affection towards younger siblings, and to when they stopped playing together. Nikki (age 9), for example, lived in a white, middle-class, nuclear family in a large city with her two younger brothers, Charlie (age 7) and Rupert (age 3). She evoked the time when the family nanny left the household and she started to dislike Charlie. She described a photograph of herself hugging Charlie when he was small in a tone of surprise:

Nikki: Well, I can't even remember this, I can't believe I did this, but when I was like five or something, or three, there's a picture where I'm hugging him, and when he's about one. It's a picture of him sitting on my lap and I'm not very old then, I'm only about three. But it's sort of like since Rupert has been born about three years ago or maybe a bit more. But since the nanny left us and we started having our parents, Mum or Dad, looking after us on school days and whatever, it started going like that. Ever since I can remember I've not liked him even though I've seen pictures of me liking him.

Interviewer: But you said that he changed a bit when your nanny left?

Nikki: Yeah, that was because she took us everywhere and we had to walk everywhere and so we got used to each other, and because we didn't go to school then it was a bit different … And I think it's also partly when you go to school you don't really see each other much, so when you're in the playground it doesn't really happen that much.

Nikki recalled the fights they used to have a few years ago and which sometimes still occurred:

We've started fighting, not as much as we did but it's – when my Mum's there we always seem to fight more and I don't know why. It doesn't happen so much now, it happens a bit now, but before, when I was seven and he was like five, that's all he was interested in doing. That's when we'd always fight, when my Mum was there, but we've stopped now.

Nikki also described her youngest brother, Rupert, as shy, but had a sense of him changing and losing his shyness as he grew older:

I used to be really shy but I'm not now. You can do stuff so it's better, you can ask people stuff. Rupert is shy and he wouldn't be able to, that's because he's younger. He'll probably get un-shy when he's older.

Michael's and Nickki's comments reflect their status as the oldest sibling in their respective families. Other children, from their perspective as a younger brother or sister, emphasised the changes they witnessed in older siblings. For example, Dan (age 11) poignantly talked about changes in his relationship with his older brother, Jamie (age 17). He lived with two older siblings and one younger in a white, working-class family in a small city. Dan felt that Jamie was distancing himself, leaving him with a sense of separation. He found it hard to talk to Jamie, who had lost interest in him. They no longer shared leisure pursuits together:

> My brother's just not interested sometimes, he doesn't really care. He's at that age, where he doesn't care … He hasn't always been like that. [It changed] when he like came to 16 … When he like took me fishing, he's not taking me fishing now, I don't know why. He says that I play up, but I don't … I feel left out.

Dan felt sad about the change to a lack of connection with Jamie. In particular, he missed the sense of being part of a collective group with his older brother.

Other children referred to change in the way that their parents perceived them as they grew up, related to age competence comparisons with their siblings, or the arrival of a new brother or sister. Some older children felt ambivalent about these imposed changes. Richard (age 12), for example, talked about how his mother seemed to regard him as old enough to look after himself. He lived in a white, middle-class step-family with his half sister, Elsa (age 4), in a large city. Since his sister's birth, Richard felt that he was expected to be competent enough to care for himself more as his parents tended to the baby. He talked about the transition to no longer being the only child:

Richard:	Well, before the attention was on me. Well, I didn't prefer that more but it sort of felt different because I was always told that I couldn't do this and I couldn't do that, but now it is sort of thought that I can just look after myself …
Interviewer:	So can you remember when Elsa was first born, can you remember how you felt?
Richard:	Yes. Well, it was quite surprising really, there was someone else there. But she was very small and she just looked like, I don't know, I felt a little bit strange and a little bit shocked because I thought everything was going to stay the same and that she is just someone else in the house, but everything changed, everything is totally different. I can't believe it … Some changes were good, like I got to see my mum

more. She used to be a nurse and I didn't used to see her much. But then she stopped thinking that I needed to be looked after, that I was the older child and I could look after myself …

Interviewer:	Do you still feel like that now?
Richard:	No. It is a bit different cos you grow older … Well, at first I thought it was going to stay the same and it didn't. Then it changed and I wondered why … I played with [Elsa] and she used to stop crying. Then she started not liking me any more. She says she liked me when she was eight but that she doesn't like me any more. But she has never been eight …

Nonetheless, some children had positive experiences of the birth of a sibling, and the opportunity to be an older brother or sister:

> I had always wanted to have a little brother or sister and at last I had one.
> (David, age 9, white, middle class)

Momentary changes

As well as change over time, many children also noted more momentary changes in their relationships with their siblings as part of their everyday lives:

> Sometimes we're friends and sometimes we hate each other … Sometimes we're friends and sometimes I don't care.
> (Kate, age 9, white, working class, talking about her older full sister, age 13)

> Sometimes he's extremely annoying when I'm trying to do my homework, but sometimes he's very kind to me and polite.
> (David, age 9, white, middle class, talking about his younger full brother, age 5)

Sudden mood changes were an instance of this kind of change in the present:

> One minute he's fine, and then the next minute [he and his friend] are like two wild cats … Sometimes he treats me good, sometimes bad.
> (Rachel, age 9, white, working class, talking about her younger full brother, age 7)

In contrast with these momentary changes, several children also reflected on the impact of memorable events that symbolised transitions in their relationships with their brothers and sisters.

Memories of significant events

Change over time for many children is linked to turning-points that marked a transition in their sibling ties. These points include remembering when an older sibling was taken into care (as for Amy, age 8) or moved away (as we discuss further in the next chapter), and sad partings and geographical divides (such as for Hlynor, age 8, in his cross-national family, discussed in Chapter 1). These changes marked the end of particular habits and routines, including the care and responsibility of an older brother or sister towards a younger one, and access to, and enjoyment of, shared leisure activities outside the home such as outings to the beach or the park, or fishing expeditions.

As we saw above, several children vividly recalled the birth of a sibling and the effect of a new brother or sister on their life. Other children attached their memories of times of change to more prosaic and everyday events. Jason (age 11), who lived in a white, working-class, lone-mother family in a village, provides an example of developmental change in relation to both his older sister, Jody (age 13) and himself:

> Jody does different things to me, but I do the same things as [my younger brother] ... Because I used to play with Jody more when I was tiny. Because, I dunno, we both used to like little baby toys and we used to play together ... [But] we got older and changed.

Natalie (age 12), from a white, working-class, nuclear family living in a city, was the second of four siblings. She described changes in her relationship with her older sister, Clara (age 16), particularly recalling the effect of Clara starting secondary school and making new friends, and the diminished intimacy and connection between them:

> When I couldn't get to sleep or something, she used to let me come and sleep in her bed and stuff, and used to like, hug and we slept together. And now it's like her in one bedroom and me in the other, because we don't really want to sleep together now. She thinks I'm a bit babyish now, because I'm not like out at all the places like she's going out with and thinks I'm babyish. [It changed] sort of when she went to senior school. And she met loads and loads of new friends and, and she was like off places with them and she didn't really go many places with her old friends. And so we sort of, I used to be upset because I never use to have anybody because my friends didn't use to come round because they were always busy, and I never used to go there often, and I didn't like it on the street.

And I was like upset because I didn't have like, I couldn't really talk to my mum about stuff cos I felt that, er, I was a bit, I felt a bit stupid. And when my sister wasn't there I was like, er, I felt a bit lonely. I feel like I'm an only child sometimes. We sort of went apart as well a bit more, and then when she went to secondary school we went apart loads.

Natalie described how she changed in response, modifying her behaviour in order to act more grown up and so attempt to better fit in with her sister's new ways, and maintain their connection:

Well I think she felt that, I think I sort of acted a bit babyish around her, to try and get her attention and stuff and then, and then I sort of realised after I was with [my friend] that I was acting like – I didn't act babyish so I'd be more friendly with her, and I'd talk like more grown up and stuff. If I, I think if I acted like that she wouldn't have wanted to go away so much … Now I'm sort of acting more grown up and stuff like that.

Continuity

In contrast to the perceptions of change in relationships discussed so far, other children experienced a sense of continuity in their sibling relationships and in their own lives. Daisy (age 9), for example, perceived changes in others, like her brother, but continuity in her own circumstances. She lived in a village in a white, nuclear, middle-class family with her older brother, Tim (age 13), who she admired as knowledgeable and a protector against bullying at school. While she saw her older brother's life changing with time – moving away and starting his own family – she saw her own as remaining static:

Daisy:	Yeah, as Tim has got older he has got more mature so he has learnt how to deal with things properly …
Interviewer:	Do you know what you will be like in the future?
Daisy:	I don't know, our personality will change, what we remember in life will change. Tim will get a girlfriend, decide to get married, decide to have children. It will be really nice … I am going to live here till I die but I think Tim will go to London. All of the best shops are there.

Other children saw age-related differences continuing even as they and their siblings grew older. In Chapter 2, we noted that Holly (age 9) saw her younger sister, Jessica's (age 5) lack of competence as an 'age thing'. She felt that Jessica would always be younger than her, and so it would always be difficult to talk to her:

Holly:	She's a bit silly about everything apart from when you feel sick. She's really funny and jokey, so she's not really that serious.
Interviewer:	Do you think that will change when you get older or will it always be like that?
Holly:	It will always be like that because she's always going to be younger than me, so it will be hard to talk to her about what's going on with me because it will be a whole lot different. Like when I need some help when I'm in Year 6, she's only going to be in Year 2, so it's going to be hard for me to talk to her about that kind of thing because she's not really going to know all about the stuff …
Interviewer:	How about when you're grown ups, can you imagine it?
Holly:	No, it's a long way away and I can't imagine it.

Conclusion

The context of time provides an important backdrop for understanding connection and separation, and status positions in children's sibling relationships, and the ways that children continually face change and transition as part of their everyday lives with their brothers and sisters. In this chapter we examined three aspects of children's understandings of change over time. These were: age-related competence, momentary changes and memories of significant events. We also looked at continuity over time as, for some children, this, rather than change, shaped their understandings of being and having a sibling.

We have shown that perceptions of change and continuity are influenced by sibling position. Older siblings can mourn or welcome the end of an era when a younger brother or sister is born, or grows out of babyhood or toddlerhood. For younger siblings, witnessing an older brother or sister growing older and moving away from them emotionally or physically can leave them feeling ambivalent. Such changes in children's sibling relationships can pose problems for them and, in the next chapter, we look at the ways that they cope with these and other difficulties.

5. Problems and coping practices

In previous chapters we have seen that – as well as strengths – children can experience problems in their relationships with their brothers and sisters. In this chapter we focus on the different coping practices that children used to deal with these difficulties. By 'coping practices' we mean the everyday actions that children use to deal with problems. Our approach to coping practices differs from the 'outsider' perspective that we discussed in Chapter 1. In these studies, professionals examine what they define as problematic sibling behaviour and offer suitable (often parent-based) solutions. Instead we focus on what children themselves defined as difficulties and the various coping practices that they told us that they used.

We begin by exploring the children's oft-used description of their siblings as 'annoying'. Children's sense of their brothers and sisters 'being annoying' is strongly related to age status and corresponding notions of maturity/immaturity and associated hierarchies within their family. Siblings are 'annoying' in a number of places – at home, at school and on the street – leading to a desire for separation from them. For some children, this desire for separation particularly occurs in the home, as we discussed in Chapter 2. In Chapter 2 we also highlighted how, for some children, arguments and fights were seen as an integral part of their feelings of connection to their siblings. For others, however, arguments and fights were regarded as problematic. Finally, we examine the issue of older siblings leaving home, and the various ways that children deal with this change in their sibling relationship. Throughout, we show that the social contexts, such as status position and gender, frame children's understandings of problems in their relationship with their brothers and sisters and their ways of dealing with them.

Being 'annoying': problematic behaviour

The term 'annoying', or variants such as 'bugs me' or 'winds me up', were used again and again by children, especially older siblings, to describe their brothers' or sisters' behaviour, or mere presence, as problematic. Older siblings' accounts suggested that their younger siblings ignored, or failed to understand, unspoken rules about space, both inside and outside the home, as well as around friends. This invasion of space within the home, their siblings' ignorance of the rules surrounding ownership of possessions, and the disruption of activities, were particularly regarded as difficulties by some older siblings:

> It was annoying cos when my friends came round here he would be annoying expecting us to play with him.
>
> *(Abbey, age 9, white, middle class, talking about her younger full brother)*

> She can be quite annoying before the bell goes because she's there and she can't go into her playground until the bell goes so she hangs around me and tries to annoy me in front of my friends.
>
> *(Holly, age 9, white, middle class, talking about her younger full sister)*

Older siblings described 'annoying' behaviour as something that is repetitive, involves noise and (excessive) movement, and is reckless and inappropriate. In contrast, the depiction of the older sibling is focused and tranquil:

> Sometimes I try and read and he just keeps talking.
>
> *(David, age 9, white, middle class, talking about his younger full brother)*

> He used to cry and it annoyed me because I couldn't get to sleep because he kept on crying.
>
> *(Jason, age 11, white, working class, talking about his younger full brother)*

> Like when I am watching TV … best programmes he screams more, shouts and runs around the room.
>
> *(Michael, age 10, Asian middle class, talking about his younger half brother)*

Annoying behaviour, for many older siblings, was associated with immaturity. Younger brothers and sisters failed to listen to people or did not respect older siblings' position of authority. They were unable to take things seriously or act 'grown up':

> Tom thinks he's the youngest of the family, he thinks that he is the baby and stuff and acts a bit like it which gets on everybody's nerves and he gets into tantrums and shuts himself in his bedroom.
>
> *(Jody, age 13, white, working class, talking about her younger full brother)*

Younger brothers and sisters rarely referred to 'annoying' behaviour in the same way as older siblings. Rather than inappropriate noisiness and lack of understanding, younger siblings were more likely to describe the 'annoyingness' of older brothers and sisters as involving inequities, getting them into trouble or physical dominance:

> Basically he blames stuff on me. Sometimes yeah, that's the kind of annoying thing that comes to mind really.
> *(Madeline, age 11, white, middle class, talking about her older full brother)*

> Cos he is annoying … Mike just hurts me. Sometimes he does stick up for me if I am crying but usually he just blames stuff on me.
> *(Bethany, age 9, white, working class, talking about her older full brother)*

Children's invocation of 'annoying' reveals a power struggle occurring between older and younger siblings. Older siblings attempted to assert themselves as more mature, and to distance themselves from the immature 'annoying' behaviour of younger siblings. As we discussed in Chapter 3, older siblings sometimes also allied themselves further up the hierarchy of their family, with parents, emphasising younger brothers' and sisters' 'babyish' behaviour. For some children, the citing of boundaries and rules of space and autonomy within the home informed a desire to separate themselves from younger siblings and their 'annoying' behaviour. Younger siblings' voices were more muted in the discussions of 'being annoying', except for when they saw themselves as positioned unfairly or subject to violence.

Being annoying: coping practices

In order to deal with annoying siblings, children used a combination of other-based (drawing on parents or other relatives) and self-based coping practices, or those involving negotiation and reasoning with their siblings.

In a number of situations, children turned to their parents to deal with 'annoying' behaviour. Most children saw this as successful or 'sometimes' successful:

> I just tell my parents and they send them all down. Then they lock the door.
> *(Bob, age 8, Asian, working class, talking about his younger full brothers coming into his room while he does his homework)*

> When I was playing with my friends yesterday I told my mum that Jessica was being really annoying so she took Jessica and told her to go and watch TV … it really sorted it out.
> *(Holly, age 9, white, middle class, talking about her younger full sister)*

In some cases, however, telling parents was not regarded as a successful coping practice; parents did not always understand 'annoying' behaviour. This was the case for John Parker (age 9), a white, middle-class boy from a nuclear family, living in a small city with his younger brother and sister. His account is suffused with the desire to be independent from his siblings and find his own space within the home:

> I tell Mummy and Daddy but they sort of go like, 'Oh, what harm is he doing?' They can't like make him stop. They don't think he is annoying so it is hard to get him to stop. [My sister] is so annoying because she sings … and my Mum, she is so annoying, they both sing. She already knows that I hate it but they don't understand that basically they just wind me up.

In John Parker's case, telling his parents failed as a coping practice; indeed his mother even contributed to the problem. As a result, he resorted to self-based ways of dealing with the problem, such as shouting at his younger brother and sister.

Other children also took the responsibility upon themselves to stop the annoying behaviour of their siblings. Children cited numerous self-based coping practices. From their accounts, the most successful of these appeared to be: ignoring the behaviour, changing activity or removing themselves. In this sense, children actively sought to control their responses, taking responsibility for diffusing tension and frustration. In contrast, they portrayed shouting and violence as serving only to aggravate the situation further:

> I just shout. But he doesn't get scared, he does it more, so then I just leave him alone. He still does it, but not as much as when you tell him not to do it.
> *(Michael, age 10, Asian, middle class, talking about his younger half brother screaming and running around the room while he watches TV)*

While children noted that 'telling' younger brothers and sisters not to be annoying was largely unsuccessful, some older siblings tried talking or explaining the problem to them. In treating younger siblings in a way that left more room for negotiation, understanding and reasoning, children felt that their younger brothers and sisters often responded more positively:

> I'd say 'I really want to go and play' … I tried that and it worked. I said 'I really want to go and play why don't you go and play with your friend Latisha?'
> *(Holly, age 9, white, middle class, talking about her younger full sister)*

> I tell him not to [disrupt my activity]. Sometimes that works, sometimes it
> doesn't. Sometimes I explain to him what I am doing and then it stops.
> *(David, age 10, white, middle class, talking about his younger full brother)*

Children could not always utilise adequate or successful coping practices to deal with
'annoying' behaviour, however, and this often led to greater conflict. It is in these
cases that younger siblings' voices become more prominent.

Arguments, fighting and 'being horrible': problematic behaviour

Arguments, fighting and being horrible stemmed from 'annoyingness' involving
conflict of interest, invasion of space and younger siblings refusing to do tasks for
older siblings. Those children who tended to emphasise fighting as normal and fun
nonetheless also said that their parents wanted them to stop arguing:

> Yes, we get big talks, big lectures about not fighting. We're told, 'Right,
> you're not going to fight and you know why you are not going to fight',
> and it goes on and on and on and you just start making these signs that
> you don't … yap yap yap.
> *(Claire, age 11, white, middle class)*

While some children attributed concerns about fighting to parents, however, many
children thought that fighting, arguing and 'being horrible' were some of the 'worst
things' about having brothers and sisters.

For younger siblings in particular, older brothers and sisters being horrible was more
problematic because they saw themselves as powerless in the situation:

> It's kind of … I like it in some ways [being the youngest], cos some people
> say the youngest can do no wrong, but cos you're younger you can get
> picked on a lot easier. The youngest seem to be not able to argue back
> easily.
> *(Ellie, age 12, white, working class, talking about her two co-resident older full and
> half sisters, and her two non-resident older half sisters)*

Children's perceptions of whose responsibility it was to stop the arguments shaped
their coping practices. For some, the responsibility was placed firmly in the hands of
parents, while others held themselves responsible for the behaviour of the sibling
group.

Figure 5.1 Sangun's (age 8) drawing of his older sisters (age 15 and 19) being horrible to him and making him cry

The worst things about having a brother or sister are...

Violence, fighting and arguments: coping practices

In cases where children cited parental wishes, they were more likely to place the responsibility for stopping fights with their parents. They wanted or expected parents to intervene and deal with arguments, and to provide the necessary resources:

> Sometime if you had like a special thing in your room where you could just, a special part of the house, which was like a cooling down room, and just have like all these activities, you could punch and just kick and do anything you like to them and nobody would really mind. The other day I was thinking 'I hate you Mark, I want a punch bag to punch you' ... so I just thought, well why don't I get a punch bag for my birthday, and then let rip on that ... Every family should have one. Save lots more fights.
> *(Claire, age 11, white, middle class)*

> | Interviewer: | Is there anything brothers and sisters can do to get along and not argue? |
> |---|---|
> | Bart: | Pay me! |
> | Zack: | Tell them if you shut up we can go to McDonald's.[3] |
> | Bart: | Have separate bedrooms! |
>
> *(Bart, age 12, and Zack, age 9, white, middle class)*

---

3 A multi-national fast food outlet.

Some children, however, appeared to have a strong sense of responsibility for their brothers and sisters in terms of dealing with fighting and arguing. In Chapter 2 we highlighted how some children felt that their siblings provided them with a feeling of being part of a collective group. This was the case for Daniel (age 9), a white, working-class boy from a step-family, who lived in a village with his older half sister (age 14) and younger full sisters (age 1 and 8). His account revealed a sense of his own and his sisters' responsibility to work together to diffuse tension. He discussed the arguments he had with his 8-year-old sister and their joint attempts to stop the fighting by physically separating themselves:

> The worst things about brothers and sisters are fighting, being rude and stuff. Cos you could hurt someone. It makes you feel bad. You shouldn't fight, it is bad … She's always arguing, and then I am always arguing, then she always comes up to me and we start to fight. And, well we don't really swear that much but it is bad to swear. You're not supposed to swear. Well we just go away from each other [to stop the fighting].

Older siblings were more likely to take responsibility for ending conflict with younger brothers and sisters by using self-based coping practices such as confronting their siblings or walking away until the conflict had subsided. Jody (age 13) was white, working class, and lived in a village with her mother and two younger brothers (age 9 and 11). Jody felt a strong responsibility for her sibling group. This sense of responsibility led her to internalise her anger, in a gendered fashion, for the good of the collective group:

> I try to not do it [be horrible to brothers when they annoy me] but if they keep on doing it then I keep on doing it, which I know I shouldn't do. It's a bit annoying really. We had an argument where he said something to me, so instead of retaliating I just ran away and pretended I didn't hear it and then I acted as though I didn't hear it for the rest of the day even though I did. We all got on better and stuff.

Younger brothers and sisters were more likely to use non-confrontational coping practices – walking away, or turning to parents or other siblings for support – to deal with conflict with their older siblings:

> Jason calls me names a few times. Sometimes I tell mum, sometimes I just run off and relax. If your older brother is picking on you, you should tell somebody, don't hit them back, call them names to their face, cos they will just hit you back and it will get worse.
>
> (Tom, age 9, white, working class, talking about his older full brother, Jason)

Younger siblings were also active in taking on the responsibility to stop arguments through non-confrontational means. Tom's account (above) also reflects the power imbalance younger siblings felt and the need to protect themselves from escalating violence. For some children, the threat of violence from older siblings was serious. Marshall (age 12) lived with his mother and baby sister in a small town. In the face of his non-resident older full brother's violence, Marshall had to adopt coping practices involving emotional and physical separation as a necessity. He did so despite desiring a closer relationship with his brother:

> I don't really speak to my brother that much [even though] he comes over here most of the time … I mean, I do love my brother [but] he always hits me. He mostly does it for fun … My brother knows I won't hit him back. It would cause too much hassle … My brother left [home], finished, bamboosh, gone, thank God, good riddance!

Siblings leaving home: a problem for siblings left behind?

Children talked about the issues involved in being separated, or living apart, from their siblings. Those who had not experienced separation were able to talk hypothetically about feelings and coping practices with the aid of a vignette. The vignette told the story of Nicki, whose older sister, Jaz, is leaving home to go to university. The children were asked whether they would give Nicki any advice and whether they had been in a similar situation.

Children articulated the type of emotions they imagined Nicki would feel or they themselves had felt when siblings left home. Feelings of 'sadness' were most commonly cited, along with a realisation that they would 'miss' them and a feeling of 'loneliness'. Some children focused on making themselves 'feel better' when older brothers and sisters left by maintaining connection through letters, emails, phone calls and text messages. Other children stressed the importance of visiting their siblings to maintain connection. The different coping practices, such as visiting siblings, asking them not to leave, or maintaining verbal and written connection, largely reflected the nature and context of children's particular sibling relationship.

Going to visit brothers and sisters who had moved away reflected the nature of the sibling relationship, particularly where it was centred around activity. As we discussed in Chapter 2, activity formed an essential part of boys' sense of connection with their siblings. A geographical distance between them and their brothers and sisters thus had the potential to erode this sense of connection, making siblings leaving home more problematic than for those children whose coping practice was to maintain connection through talking or writing. For most boys, coping practices did not include maintaining connection in this way.

Bart (age 12) and Zack (age 9) were two white, middle-class brothers living in a nuclear family in a small city. They emphasised the need to persuade older siblings not to move far away or to go with them. Their own relationship centred around activity and protection from bullies:

> Zack: [Nicki] should just try and get on with it and make some new friends and get them to be close to you and stick up for you … I think Nicki should talk to Jaz and see if she can find a different university nearer. [If it was me I would feel] upset and bored I wouldn't have anyone to wind up! You could see if you could go with them.
>
> Bart: You could find somewhere to stay where you can visit them.

Not all boys whose sibling relationships were focused on activity had an adequate coping practice to deal with the loss caused by an older sibling moving away. Thomas's (age 10) account described his failed attempts at stopping his brother moving away. He was a white, working-class boy living in a village with his mother. Thomas identified the powerlessness of younger siblings to do anything about the situation, as opposed to putting forward positive means of maintaining connection:

> Thomas: [I would feel] sad, nobody to take me to the park, nobody to take me anywhere … Just hang on and wait until [Jaz] comes up, you can't do anything about it.
>
> Interviewer: Did you try and stop [your brother leaving home] then?
>
> Thomas: Yeah, but I didn't succeed. I hid his luggage!

We have highlighted how some children felt that their siblings provided them with a feeling of being part of a collective group. For Lee (age 10), a white, working-class boy living in a nuclear family with his older brothers, in small city, this feeling of collectivity was very strong. Indeed, when the interviewer raised the topic, he was unable to imagine his older brother leaving home, or to think of an adequate coping practice to deal with the separation:

> But where would he go? What on holiday do you mean? 'Please don't go', that's what I would say.

We now look at the extent to which this disruption to the sense of being part of a collective group, as well as the loss of protective and enabling functions of older siblings, and the activity that constitute brothers' relationships, pose problems for children. We further illustrate how children's coping practices are formed in relation to gender.

Siblings leaving home: coping practices

The interruption to the collective group created by a brother or sister leaving home was not always seen as a problem by children if other people (siblings, relatives or friends) were available. Ellie (age 12) was white, working class and lived with her mother, full sister (aged 14) and half sister (age 16). Her twin half sisters (age 18) lived with their father in a nearby town. When asked whether it was important for siblings to live together, she explained:

> It doesn't always matter, it doesn't really matter. Just as long as you have some girls to help out when you need them it doesn't really matter.

Indeed, Ellie and all her sisters made explicit efforts to spend time together when they could, visiting each other.

For some girls, however, other siblings or relatives being around, and spending time together when they could, was not enough to deal with the separation from an older sister. Talk was a crucial way of dealing with the separation and maintaining connection over geographical distance. As we discussed in Chapter 2, talking was presented by girls as a significant aspect of their connection to their sisters, in contrast to the activity that constituted boys' relationships with their siblings.

Jody (quoted earlier) and her younger brother, Jason (age 11), illustrate this difference between girls' and boys' coping strategies within the same family. Their older sister, Jessica (age 25), had left home to go to university in a town some distance from the village in which they lived. Jody and her sister had a strong relationship based on talk; she said they 'talk about everything'. She offered some advice to Nicki, the child in the vignette:

> Enjoy the time [you] have got at the moment and talk to Jaz and tell her everything. My sister went to university so I couldn't see her all the time …

> she kept phoning us every night and she came to visit in the holidays and
> stuff … It was really hard at first but then it got better … I talked to Jessica,
> saying that I didn't want her to go and stuff and then if I got worried or I
> got scared then I just phoned her and it made me feel better.

Jason, however, took quite a different approach to coping with his oldest sister's
absence:

> I tried to remember that she would come back often because she used to a
> lot before she had a job. I'd tell him [Nicki] that you get used to it and
> probably she'll come down sometimes, and just remember about that. He
> could try and spend more time, if he has got any other relatives, spend
> more time with them.

Jason's approach to dealing with separation was to spend time with others, alongside
'waiting' for the connection to be revived when Jessica returned. Unlike Jody, Jason
did not appear to maintain the connection across geographical distance. As a result,
it was time that healed his feelings of:

> … sadness … because I'd hardly ever see her again … Now [Jessica's] got a
> job she doesn't come back as often but I don't mind that because I am
> getting used to it.

It is apparent from children's discussions that there is a marked gender difference in
the coping practices – or lack of them – used to deal with siblings leaving home.
Sisters appear to be substantially more resourceful in maintaining connection across
geographical distance through talk. This difference reflects the nature of girls'
relationships as centred around talk and boys' around activity. There were, of course,
exceptions to the gendered coping practices that we have identified, and so it is
important to emphasise context in children's lives.

One exception, albeit partial, is Sam (age 10), whose older half sister, Joanne
(age 19), lived in a city some distance away. Sam, who was white, middle class
and lived with his mother, had never lived with his sister. He attempted to form
connection through talk when he saw her, however, emphasising the importance
of such contact. He said that Joanne was the first person he would turn to for
advice, yet conceded that he was unable to do this because of difficulties in
contacting her:

> [I would talk to] my sister [if I had problems and needed advice]… Erm,
> well actually I wouldn't tell my sister because most of the time it is hard to
> contact her, so actually it would probably have to be mum and dad.

Conclusion

Sibling status shapes children's understandings and experiences of 'annoying' behaviour, fighting, arguing and the coping practices that they use to deal with them. When faced with younger brothers and sisters 'being annoying', older siblings often took responsibility for diffusing tension by using other-based, self-based or negotiation coping practices. Approaching parents as a coping practice had different degrees of success for children, seemingly dependent on parents' perceptions of the behaviour in question. Self-based practices were reported as similarly variably successful. The type of coping practice that involved a blurring of the boundaries of age status, where older brothers and sisters attempt to explain or negotiate with younger siblings, seemed more successful for the children who used them. Fighting was seen as a problem by both older and younger siblings. For younger siblings, however, there was the additional issue of power and the need to protect themselves from further arguments or violence, with some also feeling a responsibility for the behaviour of their sibling group. Younger brothers and sisters often felt that they were at a disadvantage in disputes.

Children's understandings of the problems surrounding older siblings moving away, in particular, highlighted marked gender differences in coping practices. Girls seem more resourceful in maintaining contact across geographical distance with sisters, than did boys. Despite this, it is clear that boys still had the same feelings of sadness and wish to maintain connection. Our discussion also reveals how, for some children, the departure of brothers or sisters was felt to be less of a problem if other relatives and friends were available. This was particularly a feature of some children's accounts, suggesting that the collective provides some siblings with an additional means of dealing with separation.

Throughout all the children's accounts, it is worth noting the absence of teachers and other professionals, or other services such as telephone helplines, as a resource to help them deal with problems in their sibling relationship. While teachers were sometimes mentioned as important people in the children's lives generally, they were never seen as someone to turn to in order to solve difficulties between brothers and sisters. This suggests that sibling problems are regarded as a 'private' family matter, even when the sibling conflict occurred at school. Other studies have also noted that children can see their family lives as 'private' matters (Edwards and Alldred 1999; Wade and Smart 2002).

Overall, the children's accounts of problems and coping practices in their sibling relationships demonstrate agency and responsibility, and the importance of social context in understanding children's perceptions of difficulties and the means that they adopt to deal with them. We discuss the implications of this in our final chapter.

6. Conclusion

In this final chapter of the report, we give an overview of the main findings of our research on children's views of their relationships with their siblings, and consider the implications for practice in a range of fields and initiatives. The findings and implications are based on the 'insider' accounts of children aged 7 to 13, who live in a variety of circumstances and are drawn from a nationally representative sample. Their understandings provide a challenge to the universalistic tenets of the majority of research on children's sibling relationships, which ignores social context and meaning, or focuses on children in 'problem' families.

The children talked to us about what it means to be and to have a sister or a brother, the strengths and drawbacks in their relationships, and the coping practices that they use to deal with difficulties and change in their daily lives. Their accounts show that children actively make sense of, and shape, their relationships with their brothers and sisters around the complex, seemingly small and taken-for-granted facets of their everyday lives together at home and in other settings, such as at school and in the neighbourhood.

Listening to children's own accounts of their lives with their brothers and sisters draws attention to how these relationships are both patterned and diverse; actively constructed by children rather than given. They allow us a glimpse into an aspect of children's family lives from their own perspective, providing a benchmark of the significance that they attach to their sibling ties, in contrast to the predominant focus on the influence of parent–child relationships.

Overview of main findings

The main messages from this study, which we discuss in turn below, highlight:

- children's complex feelings about being close to, and separate from, their brothers and sisters;
- patterns around gender and age status in how children relate to their siblings;
- everyday shifts and changes over time in children's sibling relationships; and
- the different ways in which children cope with problems in their relationships with their brothers and sisters.

Complexity in closeness and autonomy

Children's feelings of being close to and caring for their siblings, or being apart and autonomous from them, are played out around the everyday features of their lives: emotions, talk and activity, possessions, and space and place. The emotions and activities embodying connection to and separation from their brothers and sisters are important in children's sense of themselves in relation to others.

For most children, having brothers and sisters gives them a feeling that there is always 'someone there' for them. They love and care for each other. Siblings provide children with an emotional sense of protection from being alone. Children also recognise that everyday disputes occur alongside this. Some children, however, intensely dislike their siblings.

Issues of collectivity and individuality are important in sibling relationships. Some children spoke about their brothers and sisters providing them with a strong sense of identity as part of a collective group. Some saw sharing possessions and bedrooms as unremarkable. If they were parted from their siblings they often sought to integrate themselves into another group. Other children experienced themselves as individuals who were also siblings. They had a strong sense of autonomy and found it difficult to share possessions or bedroom space with their brothers and sisters.

Gender and age status patterns

Gender plays a key role in sibling relationships. Talking together is important to girls in their relationships with their sisters, while boys regard doing activities together as demonstrating closeness in their relationships with their brothers. Brother–sister relationships are based more around activity than talk. Girls feel that an inability to talk and confide in their sisters represents a sense of separation in their relationship, while boys regard a lack of shared activities with their siblings similarly. When older siblings leave home, girls seem to be more resourceful in maintaining communication and closeness across geographical distance, while boys' reliance on joint activities means that they have fewer resources to bridge the distance. These gender distinctions in modes of communication mirror studies of the production of gendered identities among children's peer groups, such as in the school setting (for example, Epstein, Kehily, Mac an Ghaill and others 2001; Frosh, Phoenix and Pattman 2002; Gordon, Holland and Lahelma 2000; James 1993; Thorne 1993).

Status based on birth order and age is influential. Being the oldest, middle or youngest sibling is more a subjective practice, however, than a technical or objective fact. It can shift as well as adhere to ascribed positions. Children often see older brothers and sisters as exercising care and protection of, as well as power over, younger siblings, for example in relation to bullying. They see younger siblings as receivers of this attention and authority. Middle siblings understand their position as a combination of being older and younger. Nevertheless, some younger siblings can also look after and protect their older brothers or sisters, or see them as immature for their age. Other children focus on equality and fairness, rather than hierarchies, in characterising their sibling relationships. The ascribed version of age status, however, most closely corresponds to aspects of the literature on sibling relationships discussed in Chapter 1 of this report (such as Mitchell 2000; Sulloway 1996, 2001).

Everyday changes over time

Past, present and future are important in how children understand their sibling relationships. Children live with everyday emotional and social change in themselves and their brothers and sisters, rather than only being confronted with change in problematic circumstances such as parental separation.

Most children are aware of changes in their own and their siblings' abilities and interests as they each grow older, and around significant events such as the birth of a younger brother or sister, or going to different schools. They also notice more momentary changes in each others' moods. Some children, however, feel a strong sense of continuity in their sibling relationships over time, even as they grow older.

Coping practices

Children use a range of coping practices to deal with difficulties in their relationships with their brothers and sisters, such as 'annoying' behaviour, arguments and fighting. They try to regulate their own behaviour, or turn to parents or other family members, or negotiate and reason with their siblings. Older siblings often take responsibility for diffusing tension, using a variety of coping practices, while younger brothers and sisters often feel that they are at a disadvantage in disputes.

Children rarely mention teachers and other professionals, or services such as telephone helplines, as a resource to help them deal with difficulties in their sibling relationships. This suggests that children regarded sibling issues as a 'private' family matter.

Implications for practice

The findings from our research show that children make sense of their sibling relationships as competent experts on their own lives. This is a reminder to practitioners that children may have different perspectives from those of adults, and that these views need to be listened to. While some areas of policy and practice highlight children's rights as important (such as parental divorce), other areas focus more on parents' responsibilities. The latter is the case both in research addressing children's sibling relationships, and in the everyday institutional and practice contexts that bear on these relationships, such as schooling and the spectrum of social care services. Children may not always know best about what decisions should be made, but they do know best about how they feel. Their perspectives need to be taken into consideration alongside those of adults, such as parents and teachers, in developing practice initiatives to support them.

Our research fills the 'gap' in knowledge about children's understandings of their sibling relationships in middle childhood. Some further issues need investigation before the relevance of our findings for practice interventions can be fully realised, however. Our sample comes from a nationally representative base, and so the number of children from minority ethnic groups in our study is limited. Since we identify social context as important, especially in relation to gender and age, it is important to explore the implications of other features of this context such as ethnicity, social class and disability.

The complexity and diversity that is evident from our research into children's experiences means that interventions that touch on children's sibling ties need to take social context into account. These relationships are not amenable to universal prescription. Furthermore, children's sense of privacy with regard to turning to people outside their family to cope with difficulties with their siblings means that interventions need to display sensitivity in this respect.

Our findings provide a benchmark for practice in working with children and supporting families in a range of professional fields and initiatives. Below we highlight several potential areas:

- the school and after-school curriculum;
- bullying prevention and other social welfare initiatives;
- parent education and family therapy; and
- looked-after children.

The school and after-school curriculum

The gendered nature of sibling relationships is relevant for educators, play leaders and practitioners in related fields. Boys' reliance on shared activities in their relationships with their brothers and sisters means that they do not always have the same communication resources available to them as girls when it comes to dealing with difficulties or change in their sibling relationships, for example when a sibling leaves home. Practice needs to take account of these different modes of communication.

Important aspects of children's sibling relationships – for example, in providing them with feelings of closeness and care, or prompting desires to be apart and autonomous, or the sense of loss that children can feel when older siblings leave home – hardly feature in relevant parts of the school curriculum, such as Personal and Social Education (PSE). These matters could be addressed in a general, rather than individual, fashion in order to respect children's feelings of privacy.

Bullying prevention and other social welfare initiatives

Siblings, both older and younger, are an unrecognised resource in initiatives to deal with bullying in the school and outside the home generally, yet they feature strongly in children's accounts. This occurs in a context where, for example, 'big brother/sister' mentoring schemes to support younger children in schools operate on the sibling model. The support that actual siblings may offer each other in cases of bullying outside the home needs to be taken into account in such initiatives.

Children have varying ideas about what is appropriate in terms of sharing with other children. Some children see joint use and ownership of possessions with siblings as unremarkable while others value individual space and possessions. Outside the home, however, children may encounter different attitudes and behaviours.

Parenting education and family therapy

Information and training aimed at parents tends either to ignore relationships between their children, or to view arguments between siblings as something to be prevented. Children usually regard arguments with their brothers and sisters as part of everyday dynamics; it is professionals, practitioners and media representations that tend to problematise conflict as rivalry. Children's understandings need to be more widely acknowledged by parent educators and parents themselves.

Children use a variety of coping practices to deal with difficulties in their relationships with their brothers and sisters. Rather than universal prescriptions about whether, and how, parents should intervene, or whether children should be left to learn to resolve their own conflicts, parent educators, family therapists and parents need to take account of children's own coping strategies and support these.

Looked-after children

Decisions about whether or not to keep sibling groups intact when children are taken into care, or the amount of contact between looked-after children and their brothers and sisters who live elsewhere, need to take careful account of children's sibling relationships. The complexity and diversity of children's sibling relationships revealed in this study show that what is appropriate for one child or sibling group may not be appropriate for another, and that it is important to pay attention to social context in making decisions about sibling contact on children's behalf.

Conclusion

This report presents children's views of their sibling relationships in middle childhood. Children's accounts offer new insights in providing supportive intervention for family relationships. Their views add to our knowledge of family lives, and need to be heard alongside and in interaction with those of other family members. In the case of sibling relationships, however, neither the topic itself nor the views of children have received much attention. Yet, as our findings show, children's relationships with their brothers and sisters are significant. They constitute a key aspect of their everyday lives inside and outside the home.

Listening to children reveals that sibling relationships are complex and diverse, rather than universally ascribed and amenable to prescription; patterned according to social context and actively understood and shaped by children themselves. The accounts of the children in this research – drawn from a nationally representative sample, rather than focusing on children in problematic circumstances – provide an everyday benchmark of children's relationships with their brothers and sisters. They show us that sibling relationships form an important part of childhood. Brothers and sisters give children feelings of being cared for and about, forming a supportive resource just as much as they can present difficulties and problems.

References

Bank, S. and Kahn, M. (1982) *The Sibling Bond*. New York: Basic Books.

Borland, M., Laybourn, A., Hill, M. and Brown, J. (1998) *Middle Childhood: The Perspectives of Children and Parents*. London: Jessica Kingsley.

Brannen, J., Heptinstall, E. and Bhopal, K. (2000) *Connecting Children: Children's Views of Family Life*. London: Falmer Press.

Brody, G.H., Stoneman, Z.J. and Burke, M. (1987) 'Child temperaments, material differential behaviour and sibling relationships', *Developmental Psychology*, 23(3), pp 354–62.

Cawson, P., Wattam, C., Brooker, S. and Kelly, G. (2000) *Child Maltreatment in the United Kingdom: A Study of the Prevalence of Child Abuse and Neglect*. London: NSPCC.

Chamberlain, M. (1999) 'Brothers and sisters, uncles and aunts: a lateral perspective on Caribbean families', in E.B. Silva and C. Smart (eds) *The New Family?* London: Sage.

Duncan, R. (1999) 'Peer and sibling aggression: an investigation of intra- and extra- familial bullying', *Journal of Interpersonal Violence*, 14(8), pp 871–87.

Dunn, J. (1988) *The Beginnings of Social Understanding*. Oxford: Blackwell.

Dunn, J. and Deater-Deckard, K. (2001) *Children's Views of Their Changing Families*. York: York Publishing Services/Joseph Rowntree Foundation.

Dunn, J. and Plomin, R. (1990) *Separate Lives: Why Siblings Are So Different*. New York: Basic Books.

Edwards, R. (2002) 'Creating "stability" for children in step-families: time and substance in parenting', *Children & Society*, 16, pp 154–67.

Edwards, R. and Alldred, P. (1999) 'Children and young people's views of social research: the case of research on home–school relations', *Childhood*, 6(2), pp 261–81.

Elgar, M. and Head, A. (1999) 'An overview of siblings', in A. Mullender (ed.) *We Are Family: Sibling Relationships in Placement and Beyond*. London: British Agencies for Adoption and Fostering.

Epstein, D., Kehily, M.J., Mac an Ghaill, M. and Redman, P. (2001) 'Boys and girls come out to play: making masculinities and femininities in school playgrounds', *Men and Masculinities*, 4, pp 158–72.

Frosh, S., Phoenix, A. and Pattman, R. (2002) *Young Masculinities*. London: Palgrave.

Furman, W.C. and McQuaid, E.L. (1992) 'Intervention programs for the management of conflict', in W.W. Hartup (ed.) *Conflict in Child and Adolescent Development*. New York, NY: Cambridge University Press.

Gordon, T., Holland, J. and Lahelma, E. (2000) *Making Spaces: Citizenship and Difference in Schools*. Basingstoke: Macmillan.

Graham, M.J. (1999) 'The African-centred world view: developing a paradigm for social work', *British Journal of Social Work*, 29(2), pp 251–67.

Hair, E., Jager, J. and Garrett, S. (2001) *Background for Community Level Work on Social Competency in Adolescence: Reviewing the Literature on Contributing Factors*. Washington, DC: John S. and James L. Knight Foundation.

Hall, J. (1997) 'Children in step-families', in *Unhappy Families, Unhappy Children: A ChildLine Study*. London: ChildLine.

Iacovou, M. (2001) *Fertility and Female Labour Supply*. Institute for Social and Economic Research (ISER) Working Paper 2001-19, University of Essex.

James, A. (1993) *Childhood Identities: Self and Social Relationships in the Experience of Children*. Edinburgh: Edinburgh University Press.

James, A., Jenks, C. and Prout, A. (1998) *Theorising Childhood*. Cambridge: Polity Press.

Kosonen, M. (1999) '"Core" and "kin" siblings', in A. Mullender (ed.) *We Are Family: Sibling Relationships in Placement and Beyond*. London: British Agencies for Adoption and Fostering.

Kramer, L., Perozynski, L.A. and Chung. T. (1999) 'Parental responses to sibling conflict: the effects of development and parent gender', *Child Development*, 70, pp 402–29.

Laviola, M. (1992) 'Effects of older brother–younger sister incest: a study of the dynamics of 17 cases', *Child Abuse and Neglect*, 16(3), pp 409–21.

Lockwood, R., Gaylord, N., Kitzmann, K. and Cohen, R. (2002) 'Family stress and children's rejection by peers: do siblings provide a buffer?', *Journal of Child and Family Studies*, 11(3), pp 331–45.

Mason, A. (1997) 'Standard families: their troubles', in *Unhappy Families, Unhappy Children: A ChildLine Study*. London: ChildLine.

Mauthner, M. (2002) *Sistering: Power and Change in Female Relationships*. Basingstoke: Palgrave.

Mayall, B. (2002) *Towards a Sociology for Childhood: Thinking From Children's Lives*. Buckingham: Open University Press.

McNamee, S. (1999) ' "I won't let her in my room" – sibling strategies of power and resistance', in J. Seymour and P. Bagguley (eds) *Relating Intimacies*. London: Macmillan.

Meadows, S. (1990) *The Child as Thinker*. London: Routledge.

Mitchell, J. (2000) *Mad Men and Medusas: Reclaiming Hysteria and the Effects of Sibling Relationships on the Human Condition*. London: Penguin Books.

Mitchell, J. (2003) *Siblings: Sex and Violence*. Cambridge: Polity Press.

Mok, C. and Bromfield, N. (undated) 'Parents as third parties to children's disputes', PowerPoint presentation, available online: www.psychology.uwaterloo.ca/courses/Psych453/3rdPartyParents.ppt

Morrow, V. (1998) *Understanding Families: Children's Perspectives*. York: Joseph Rowntree Foundation.

Morrow, V. (2003) 'Perspectives on children's agency within families: a view from the sociology of childhood', in L. Kuczynski (ed.) *Handbook of Dynamics in Parent–Child Relations*. Thousand Oaks, CA: Sage Publications.

Mullender, A. (1999) 'Sketching in the background', in A. Mullender (ed.) *We Are Family: Sibling Relationships in Placement and Beyond*. London: British Agencies for Adoption and Fostering.

Office for National Statistics (2001) *Census 2001*. www.statistics.gov.uk

Patterson, G.R. (1986) 'The contribution of siblings to training for fighting: a microsocial analysis', in D. Olweus, J. Block and M. Radke-Yarrow (eds) *Development of Antisocial and Prosocial Behaviour: Research, Theory and Issues*. New York: Academic Press.

Phinney, J. (1989) 'Stages of ethnic identity development in minority group adolescents', *Journal of Early Adolescence*, 9, pp 34–49.

Platt, L. (2002) *Parallel Lives? Poverty Amongst Ethnic Minority Groups*. London: Child Poverty Action Group.

Richman, N., Stevenson, J. and Grayham, P. (1982) *Preschool to School: A Behavioural Study*. London: Academic Press.

Siddiqi, A. and Ross, H.S. (1999) 'Roles and resolutions: the way sibling conflict ends', *Journal of Early Education and Development*, 10, pp 315–32.

Steelman, L.C., Powell, B., Werum, R. and Carter, S. (2002) 'Reconsidering the effects of sibling configuration: recent advances and challenges', *Annual Review of Sociology*, 28, pp 243–69.

Stocker, C. and Dunn, J. (1994) 'Sibling relationships in childhood and adolescence', in R. Plomin (ed.) *Nature and Nurture During Middle Childhood*. Malden, MA: Blackwell Publishers.

Sulloway, F. (1996) *Born to Rebel: Birth Order, Family Dynamics and Creative Lives*. New York: Pantheon.

Sulloway, F. (2001) 'Sibling order'. www.sulloway.org

Terwogt, M.M. and Harris, P.J. (1993) 'Understanding of emotion', in M. Bennet (ed.) *The Child as Psychologist*. Hemel Hempstead: Harvester Wheatsheaf.

Thorne, B. (1993) *Gender Play: Boys and Girls in Schools*. Buckingham: Open University Press.

Wade, A. and Smart, C. (2002) *Facing Family Change: Children's Circumstances, Strategies and Resources*. York: York Publishing Service.

Woolfson, R. (2002) *Siblings: Encouraging Them to be Friends*. London: Hamlyn.

Index